THE
HAPPINESS
HACK

Praise for THE HAPPINESS HACK

"In today's stressful, complex world, who among us wouldn't benefit from a happiness boost? Ellen Leanse breaks down the process of achieving happiness with understandable and useful examples that merge brain science and well-researched wisdom in this approachable, fascinating, helpful book. A must read!"

—LYNDA WEINMAN, EDUCATOR AND COFOUNDER OF LYNDA.COM

"*The Happiness Hack* is a user's manual for the brain. It makes neuroscience understandable, relevant, and practical, providing a friendly, actionable guide to putting your brain to work for you."

—NIR EYAL, BESTSELLING AUTHOR OF *HOOKED: HOW TO BUILD HABIT-FORMING PRODUCTS*

"As a neuroscientist, I'm always thinking about ways to get knowledge about the brain 'out of the lab' and into the hands of people who can use it to improve their lives. Ellen does that with *The Happiness Hack*. It makes knowledge about the brain relevant and accessible while offering ways to apply insights from neuroscience to positive changes in everyday life."

—SARAH EAGLEMAN, PHD, NEUROSCIENTIST

"If you want to be more happy, productive, calm, and fulfilled (and who doesn't?), then this is the book for you. Wisdom and wonder burst out of every page, along with clear and simple explanations of the science behind what goes on in our heads. Your life—and your brain—will never be the same again."

—ROZ SAVAGE, GUINNESS WORLD RECORD HOLDER AND LECTURER AT YALE UNIVERSITY

THE
HAPPINESS
HACK

How to Take Charge of Your Brain and Create More Happiness in Your Life

Ellen Petry Leanse

for Alex, Jeff, and Matt—
always my best teachers

To enjoy good health, to bring TRUE HAPPINESS to one's family, to bring peace to all, one must first DISCIPLINE and CONTROL one's own mind. If we can control our mind, we can find the way to Enlightenment, and all WISDOM and VIRTUE will naturally come to us.

—THE BUDDHA

HAPPINESS is not a station
you arrive at, but a
manner of TRAVELING.

—MARGARET LEE RUNBECK, NOVELIST

Nothing captures the biological argument better than the famous New Age slogan: "HAPPINESS BEGINS WITHIN." Money, social status, plastic surgery, beautiful houses, powerful positions—none of these will bring you happiness. Lasting happiness comes only from serotonin, dopamine, and oxytocin.

—YUVAL NOAH HARARI, *SAPIENS: A BRIEF HISTORY OF HUMANKIND*

Take a second.
Think whatever you want.
IT'S YOUR BRAIN. Make
yourself at home in it.

—LIN-MANUEL MIRANDA,
PLAYWRIGHT, COMPOSER, ACTOR

Contents

Introduction

A FEW YEARS BACK, I faced some big questions and daunting struggles. No one would have guessed it: I hid my worries well. But something was off, and I felt alone in my questions. Looking around, it seemed other people had answers I simply couldn't find. Watching them, I wondered what I was missing.

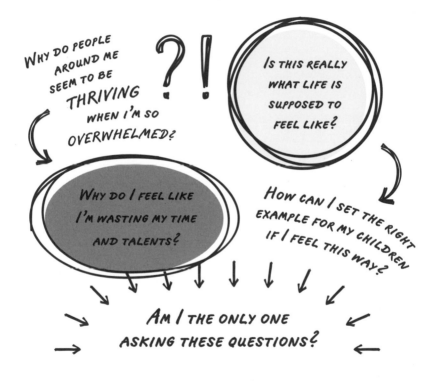

I didn't know where to find answers. After all, these aren't questions people bring up in casual conversation. Around me, it seemed, people were doing great—at least that's what they told me. So I smiled harder and pretended it all made sense to me too.

I felt more than confused.

I felt alone.

When I talked with my doctor about my concerns, he shrugged and said, "Everyone feels this way." Maybe he thought I'd find this revelation comforting. I didn't. He talked about medications he usually prescribed when people shared these feelings.

"Really?" I wondered. "Is that the answer?"

Something inside told me there was another way. So I went looking for it. I opened my mind and challenged my assumptions. I read voraciously, took classes, and explored every path I could to learn how others answered life's tough questions about meaning, purpose, and the pursuit of happiness. I looked to philosophy, modern and timeless wisdom, and science. I studied anthropology and religion. I explored real-life stories and tried to increase my self-expression and self-care.

Insights came slowly at first. But when I started learning about the brain, something clicked. For the first time, I saw patterns across the different paths to happiness—and even in my own experiences. With increasing clarity, I saw a new light. Neuroscience—the science of the brain—seemed to reveal some of the answers I was seeking. And the more I learned, the clearer those answers became.

Today, I still have questions. But they're about what's possible, not about what's holding me back. As I've learned to work with my brain—and studied its role in shaping our life experiences—I'm happier. More energized. More curious, focused, and confident, beyond what I would have imagined a few years back. Nothing could have prepared me for the benefits I've received by learning to understand, and work in accord with, my brain.

As I've shared my learning with students and audiences in Silicon Valley and beyond, I see again and again how understanding the brain and working with it—in a word, being mindful—helps us do more of what satisfies us and less of what slows us down.

This book offers some of the frameworks that have helped me, and people I've worked with, find more purpose, clarity, and satisfaction. As I talk with people—all kinds of people, from different backgrounds and experiences, whether they've lived with ease or faced real hardship—their questions sound surprisingly like mine did ten years ago. My intention in writing this book is to offer you a shorter path than my process gave me. Navigating unknown terrain was hard, but now that I have a map, I want to share it.

Understanding the brain helps give you some control of it, at least some of the time, rather than simply letting it be in charge of you. Brain-aware thinking helps you take charge of an incredibly powerful tool, guiding you to new paths—to focus, a sense of purpose, and even happiness. As you'll learn in the pages ahead, working *with* your brain gives you new ways to face life with clarity and resilience.

Getting to Know
YOUR BRAIN

Your brain is built of cells called neurons and glia—hundreds of billions of them. Each one of these cells is as complicated as a city... Each cell sends electrical pulses to other cells, up to hundreds of times per second. If you represented each of these trillions and trillions of pulses in your brain by a single photon of light, the combined output would be blinding.

The cells are connected to one another in a network of such staggering complexity that it bankrupts human language and necessitates new strains of mathematics... There are as many connections in a single cubic centimeter of brain tissue as there are stars in the Milky Way galaxy.

—DAVID EAGLEMAN, *INCOGNITO: THE SECRET LIVES OF THE BRAIN*

Your Brain: An Owner's Guide

Inside your head is a three-pound marvel that rivals any technology in the world today. Sparked by the flow of electrical currents and an ever-changing blend of chemicals, each with a distinct job, it unendingly updates and remaps itself to make *you* possible.

Powered by one hundred billion neurons, each connected to ten thousand additional neurons, the brain, many say, is the most complex object in the known universe. And what a job it does!

It regulates your fundamental body functions: your breath, heart rate, and digestion. It regulates sleep, hunger, growth, and hormonal cycles.

It processes memories. Emotions. Cravings, and how you indulge them. It manages how you sense and navigate the world. All this, and an unending list beyond, is the work of your brain, often without you even knowing what it's up to.

Your brain also does things you're very much aware of. It lets you carefully place a bandage on a child's knee, mindfully directing muscle movements that otherwise simply happen. It guides how you close your eyes and inhale slowly when you smell something delicious, savoring the aromas—and the moment.

When you organize how you'll study for a test, consider why you should (or shouldn't) get a puppy, carefully explain a process to a new employee, or stop yourself from losing your temper, you guessed it: you're also using your brain.

But you're using different brain functions, and even different brain areas, for the various actions just described.

Our brains are so complex it's hard to explain them in any one description. They remain mysterious, even with ever-advancing work in neuroscience and other cognitive sciences: linguistics, psychology, anthropology, artificial intelligence, philosophy, and more. Textbooks, websites, even popular shows explore the brain's intricacies. Yet no one discipline seems to give us a full understanding of how our brains really work—*or* how we can work with them.

To begin to understand the brain, we could take an anatomical approach, reviewing the brain's specific regions and each of their unique roles. We could explore the chemistry of the brain, discussing how neurotransmitters and hormones modulate brain activity. We could look to psychology, studies of consciousness, or other disciplines seeking to understand life through the perspective of the brain.

All of these ways are fascinating. No one path, though, does the whole job. To paint a full picture, this book borrows from a range of disciplines—neuroscience, psychology, spirituality, anthropology, and more. It shares wisdom from great thinkers, from respected leaders, and from a range of artists and innovators who've left meaningful marks on the world. We'll look at all of this through the lens of happiness, sharing enough about the brain to ignite new ways of thinking about it as you make decisions about your life—and your path to satisfaction.

In the pages ahead:

WE'LL LOOK AT BASIC BRAIN ANATOMY TO SHOW WHERE SOME OF THE THINGS WE TALK ABOUT ARE HAPPENING;

WE'LL PEEK AT A FEW BRAIN CHEMICALS: THE MAIN ONES SPARKING FEELINGS OF PLEASURE, MOTIVATION, STRESS, AND SATISFACTION;

WE'LL EXPLORE THE BRAIN'S INNATE PROCESSES: HOW IT MAKES DECISIONS AND HOW, IN SOME CASES, WE CAN AFFECT OR ALTER ITS AUTOMATIC RESPONSES; AND

WE'LL EXPLORE WHY THE BRAIN DEFAULTS TO FAMILIAR ROUTINES, EVEN WHEN THEY MAY NOT LEAD TO THE THOUGHTS OR ACTIONS WE WISH WE COULD CHOOSE.

The point of this book is to give you a glimpse of what's going on inside your head so you can work with your brain's tendencies and potential in new ways. Your brain, after all, is something of a "prediction machine," working nonstop to keep you safe and alive.

It constantly updates itself with incoming information from the world around you and integrates those updates to the vast stores of information collected across your entire life experience. When new information comes in, the brain calls on existing, dependable pathways, or maps, to guide its response. Left to itself, it will stick, often stubbornly, to those well-worn pathways—even if they're not leading us in the desired direction.

That can make change hard. It's almost as if the brain is saying, "If it's worked so far, keep doing it. If it's new, it's risky—so resist."

"Worked," to the brain, is pretty simple. For the brain, if you're here, you've survived, so what you've done in the past must be working. Regardless of how happy your past decisions, outlooks, or actions have made you, to the brain, it's been a winning strategy.

But, as this book will explain, you can often have a say in which pathways the brain uses, or even paves: the old familiar go-tos or new ones you choose. What's more, as you choose new ways, moving from automatic decisions to intentional ones, your brain will continue to update its pathways. With time, those pathways will become part of your brain's map of "what works," helping those once-new actions become easy, even automatic, routines.

To start understanding this, let's look at some brain basics.

Your Brain = The Digital World

One zettabyte of information: it even *sounds* like a lot. And it is. In fact, it's so big, we have to describe it in ways most of us have never imagined before. Haven't heard of a zettabyte? You're not alone: it's a term recently coined to describe the amount of digital information stored in the world today.

But that's how much information it would take to plot a three-dimensional map of just one brain's wiring. According to Princeton computational neuroscientist Sebastian Seung, who creates "slice images" of human brains to map the way neurons connect in the brain, it would take a full zettabyte of information—the equivalent of *all digital information in the world*—to reveal the wiring between all of the connections.[1]

A byte, you may know, is a unit of digital information. A letter, number, or character generally takes up one byte of computer memory.

A zettabyte is 1,000,000,000,000,000,000,000 bytes.

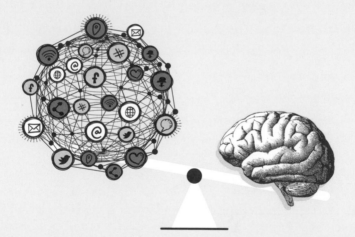

For reference, it would take seventy-five billion sixteen-gigabyte iPads to store a zettabyte of information.

Your brain may weigh only three pounds, but it truly is among the most complicated objects in the world.

1   James Gorman, "All Circuits Are Busy," *New York Times*, May 26, 2014, https://www .nytimes.com/2014/05/27/science/all-circuits-are-busy.html?_r=0.

Brain Basics

We can cluster the brain's functions into three basic categories.

MANAGING OUR BODIES: THE HINDBRAIN

The brain, obviously, largely controls the body. It directs operations we're not always aware of (like heart or breathing rate) or

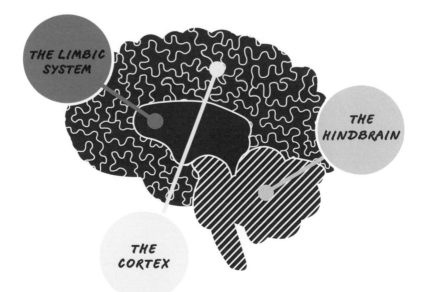

THE LIMBIC SYSTEM

THE HINDBRAIN

THE CORTEX

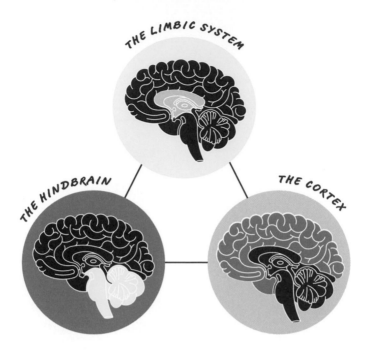

don't know how to be aware of (try activating your spleen to see for yourself). It regulates appetite and sleep cycles, and guides our biological desires to eat or sleep. It also coordinates digestive processes, balance, and hormone levels.

These functions and countless others integrate across many different parts of the brain. However, generally speaking, the body-oriented parts of our brains span the regions stacked on the spinal column from the back of our necks to the center of the brain.

The body management parts of the brain are the most ancient and the ones most similar to other animals' brains. Their functions are highly efficient and largely invisible to us: we are neither conscious of nor in control of most of their work. As we move up and toward the forehead, the brain areas become more distinctly human, and less autonomous, in their processing.

HOUSING MEMORIES AND EMOTIONS:
THE LIMBIC SYSTEM

Feelings and memories are essential tools for navigating human life. They're so important the brain manages them in a dedicated center: the limbic system, a fist-sized region nestled around the central core of the brain.

The limbic system's location hints at how integrated it is with both body and cognitive processes. Humans are social animals. Our ability to interact with others, and to use feelings to guide our actions, helped early humans survive. Memories, sensitivities, and responses—personal perspectives inform our relationship to the world around us, even without our awareness. We may not realize it, but our memories and emotions guide the way we make sense of, and take action in, our moment-to-moment experiences.

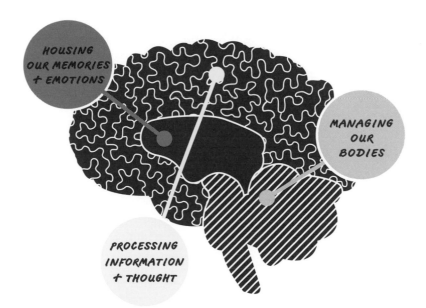

HOUSING
OUR MEMORIES
+ EMOTIONS

MANAGING
OUR
BODIES

PROCESSING
INFORMATION
+ THOUGHT

Layers upon Layers

Have you ever made a rubber band ball? You take the rubber bands found wrapped around newspapers, bunches of carrots, or holding your shoeboxes closed—maybe even one the schoolyard bully shot at you from across the playground—and wrap them around each other, building outward.

Maybe you started with a pebble in the center. Maybe a little wad of paper. Or maybe just a first rubber band. And you keep building, for weeks, months, even years. After a while, you may not recall what's at the center of the ball. But it's still there, affecting every layer wrapped around it.

So it goes with memories and emotions. Some are on the surface, visible to you and easy to identify. Some are hidden a bit beneath, not entirely visible or identifiable—but as important to the way you (and your brain!) navigate your experiences as they are to the structure of that rubber band ball.

Psychologically speaking, that's kind of how the brain builds memories and emotions. We layer new perceptions upon old ones, even upon old ones we can't see. Knowing what's on the outside is one thing; often, we're aware of the newer stuff. It's the older stuff that tends to go invisible.

Yet we build our new memories and emotions upon them. Even when we don't sense or remember what's hidden inside, they're there.

PROCESSING INFORMATION AND THOUGHT: THE CORTEX

The brain processes massive amounts of information from emotions, the senses, prior learning, and much more as it directs what to do next. This is the work of the cortex, that lumpy outer covering we often think of when we visualize the brain. Although common images of the brain tend to show it as a continuous assembly of wrinkly tissue, the cortex is actually made up of numerous domains, each with specific functions. Sensory information from the outside world, language, perception, thought, and more are all processed here.

Most of this processing—as much as 90 percent, according to some theories—happens without our awareness. The brain takes everything it's mapped so far and calculates, in an instant, how to react.

Only a fraction of our thinking is actually intentional in the "thoughtful and aware" sense. Why? Well, the brain is made to act fast. After all, speedy decisions—ones we don't even have to "think" about—have saved our ancestral bacon since the dawn of time.

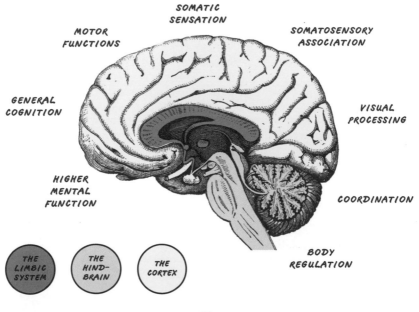

Yet some of our brains' fast decisions may not be the ones we'd choose if we had, or took, time to think about them. With due respect to the brain's ability to act fast, there are times when the speedy reaction isn't the best. Think about the moments when you've snapped at a friend, blurted out the wrong answer, or chomped down that extra slice of pizza, and you'll sense how unintentional the brain's fast decisions can be.

Fast thinking—often the automatic repetition of actions you've frequently taken or thoughts you've had—is the brain's "go to" pattern. But it doesn't always lead to our most satisfying outcomes.

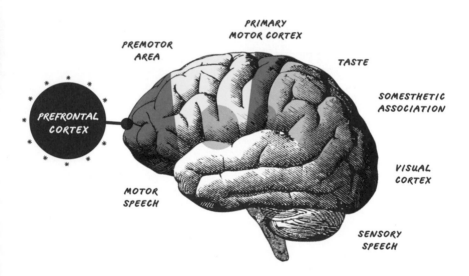

For those, we need to shift gears, and that takes awareness and effort. Intentional or mindful thinking is slower, less efficient, and less habitual than the brain's usual routines. Yet this sort of thinking often leads to more satisfying long-term results than routine reactions deliver. Generally speaking, intentional process-ing happens in the most recently evolved part of the human

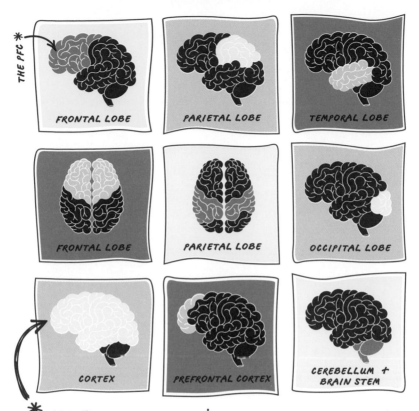

CORTEX: MOST OF THE BRAIN'S REAL ESTATE IS DEDICATED TO THIS INFORMATION-PROCESSING CAPACITY. WHAT WE GENERALLY SEE IN A PICTURE OF THE BRAIN—THAT GRAY, WRINKLY, BICYCLE HELMET–SHAPED STUFF? THAT'S WHERE INFORMATION PERCEPTION AND PROCESSING HAPPENS. THIS AREA, GENERALLY CALLED THE CORTEX, OCCUPIES ABOUT 75 PERCENT OF THE BRAIN'S MASS. IN THE CORTEX, YOU'LL FIND EVERYTHING YOU NEED TO SENSE AND MAKE SENSE OUT OF THE OUTSIDE WORLD, ALONG WITH THE AREAS YOU CALL ON WHEN THINGS DON'T MAKE SENSE. IN OTHER WORDS, IT'S WHERE YOU RECEIVE, INTEGRATE, PROCESS, AND DECIDE HOW TO ACT ON INFORMATION IN BOTH FAST (ROUTINE) AND SLOW (INTENTIONAL) WAYS.

brain: the prefrontal cortex, or PFC. The PFC occupies the area behind your forehead. Rest your palms at your temples, fingers pointing in, and you'll pretty much cover its territory. The PFC is the home of complex cognition including planning, critical thought, and impulse control. It's where we make conscious decisions and evaluate trade-offs, and where we find ways to resist the easy actions and choose the ones we really want.

These types of thinking are often referred to as "higher cognitive functions." They're the willful thoughts we hold in our minds and reflect on when we mindfully direct decisions rather than let the brain's automatic processes decide for us.

Although we can roughly describe the functions of the brain within these three contexts—body management, emotional and memory processing, and interpreting information and thought, it's not quite that simple. The brain is a complex, cohesive system. It integrates information from multiple areas to perform even relatively simple processes. This three-part framework paints a general picture of what the brain does, and where it does it, so you can apply that understanding in the chapters ahead.

Mindfulness

"Mindful" is a word often applied to willful or intentional thinking: that "held in mind" thought we direct to the prefrontal cortex. We can think of mindfulness as the act of interrupting the brain's tendency toward routine, reactive, and fast processing. Instead, we shift, intentionally, to aware, directed thinking.

Consider the basic brain areas and their functions: managing bodily functions, housing memory and emotion, and processing information.

All three of these modes work together and simultaneously. We can flow, shift, or even be jolted from one mode to another. For the most part, our body functions are invisible to us: completely autonomous. Normally, for example, we don't think about breathing. But we can. We can control our breathing rate, or hold our breath. We can learn to breathe differently (think swimming or meditation) to the point where it becomes unconscious or even automatic to breathe that way. But most of the time, breathing, like other bodily functions, happens at a level that we don't, and even can't, control.

Memory, emotion, perception, and thought are different. Although generally these levels of processing are unconscious, we have a different level of agency with them than we do, say, with the way we breathe while we're asleep.

We can, for example, work our way back to memories or feelings and gain insight into how they affected us. We can practice managing our emotions, finding new ways to process things like anger, sadness, negativity, or fear. We can train our perceptions, learning to tune out background noise, overcome a fear of heights, or enjoy spicy foods.

We can also learn to be aware of our thoughts (some of them, at least), shifting them to where we can control them rather than letting them mindlessly control us.

A fun way to think about this is by imagining two cars. One is an engineering marvel: a full-featured, fast, automated beauty loaded with bells and whistles. Generally speaking, it runs in driverless mode, managing speed, monitoring traffic, optimizing your route, and alerting you when it needs something. But you don't really have to think about it. You're simply along for the ride.

Now, sometimes you'd override that car if you wanted to. If a scenic vista caught your eye as you cruised down the highway, you could flip the turn signal and pull over to take in the view.

But unless you took action, that car would keep rolling on. It wouldn't be concerned with helping you enjoy the scenery. It would work to get you where you're going, on time—and to keep you safe as you got there.

Then, imagine another car: a slow-moving off-road vehicle that guzzled gas, needed regular maintenance, and took work to get started—but got you to places you couldn't reach any other way.

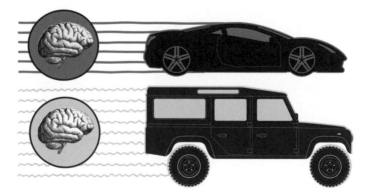

If you could, you'd flip between these cars for different drives. You'd slide into the driverless car for everyday commutes, letting it do the work so you could relax while it navigated the road.

Sometimes you'd override it, challenging the preprogrammed agenda and taking a different route than it suggested, then letting it take over again.

Yet for some drives, you'd fire up that off-road buggy and put your hands on the wheel, pointing it exactly where you wanted to go. You'd feel confident it was up to the job, despite the work it took to drive. You'd know it had the features and functions to get you places that sleek cruiser could never go.

But you might check the oil first.

Here's some good news: both of those vehicles are parked in your cranial garage.

There's even better news. These two vehicles tend to travel together, ready for you to shift—or be shifted—between them, depending on your needs. Normally, the driverless car would own the road, cruising along without needing a thing from you. Now and again it might come across a bumpy passage, or a place without an available map. Then it would shift things over to the off-road vehicle, shifting back once the tricky part had been navigated.

Generally speaking, a driverless car doesn't really need a driver. The person in the driver's seat is actually more of a passenger.

Sometimes, though, a driver wants something different from its car's preprogrammed plan, familiar and efficient as that it may be. There's scenery to notice. A path less followed that's about something more than getting there fast. Or simply the skill and enjoyment of driving a hands-on car and getting better at it with practice.

So it goes with our brains. Most of the time, they're driverless: automatically following the programmed routes.

The thing is, the routes they've learned and optimized may not be the ones the driver wants to keep traveling. Sometimes we want to take back the wheel and head in a different direction, tricky as the gears might feel at first.

This kind of driving puts the skill, and the work, into the hands of the driver.

Try It Out

Take a cookie break while you think about this, even if it's only with an imaginary cookie. Grab one, fast, and chomp into it. By the time the cookie is gone, you'll barely even know you've eaten it.

Next, take a nice little bite, maybe while you look out your window at the view outside. Pay attention to the scenery and the taste of the cookie. Sip some coffee and savor the contrast in flavors.

Then, slow down and take an even smaller bite, examining the texture on your teeth and layers of subtle flavors melting on your tongue.

That's what it's like to shift gears, exploring the range of awareness we can bring to an experience—and sensing the transitions between brain modalities.

Who Runs the Show?

The brain runs the show, right? Isn't that what it's for?

Well, if you're in that driverless car, then yes: the brain is in charge. Managing your body and processing some 90 percent of thoughts and actions? Thank goodness we're in a state-of-the-art cruiser for that amount of work.

After all, the brain is a hungry organ. Although it occupies only 2 percent of our adult body mass, it consumes some 20 percent of our energy supply. It runs on glucose (metabolized sugar) and oxygen, and it's ravenous for both. Take either away, even for a moment, and the brain slows down. Go longer, and there's actual danger. Drops in glucose correlate with problems in thinking, memory, and impulse control. Lack of oxygen? We know those dangers. Four to six minutes without oxygen and the brain suffers irreversible damage—or even death.

By operating efficiently, the brain conserves glucose and oxygen, keeping it available for whatever might be coming around the bend. So it operates in automatic mode whenever it can. In other words, it runs the show.

But if you're shifting to that other car, something else seems to take over. That thing seems to take charge, at least when it can get behind the wheel.

Mindfulness activates that thing, whatever it is. It takes some of the control away from the programmed processes and puts it in the

The **MIND** controls the
BRAIN controls the mind.

—DAVID ROCK, AUTHOR, FOUNDER OF
THE NEUROLEADERSHIP INSTITUTE

hands of a "driver": one with an intention or agenda that can differ from what the automatic car would choose.

Many religious, spiritual, and psychological traditions talk about this driving force. Some call it the mind. Some may say the spirit, or the soul; some the superego. Others assert that the force is simply another brain function. These differing voices can agree to only one thing: that no one really knows.

And we don't have to know. Yet one practice, Buddhism, offers a friendly term to describe this force: the Watcher. This is a simple reference to "whatever it is" that watches our thoughts and actions, but is separate from those thoughts and actions. Like the passenger or driver of those cars, sometimes it's active and sometimes it's not. Sometimes it's along for the ride and sometimes it owns the road. In either mode, it can be watchful and aware. Passively or actively, the Watcher is mindful.

Putting the Watcher on Watch

The Watcher sounds useful, right? Something that directs us to awareness, guides big-picture thinking, and coaches us to say, "But, on the other hand…"

It *is* useful. We all have examples of times when we did our best work by resisting the easy, default approach (like that automatic car's programmed route) and thought through a better way. We feel good about those moments and less so about the times when we acted fast, reacted automatically, and regretted the consequences later.

But the Watcher can't be on duty full-time. Think of the Watcher as a highly paid worker. "Watcher" thinking activates the

WATCHING, OBSERVING

"The Watcher," or, as it's often called, "the observing mind," refers to the inherent knowing capacity of AWARENESS. Sometimes in teaching MINDFULNESS, this is spoken of as a separate thing, as in "You can cultivate the observing mind."

More accurately, it's a function of what we call mind or CONSCIOUSNESS...not the thinking mind, but awareness itself: the mind that knows.

—PAMELA WEISS, ZEN BUDDHIST TEACHER AND COACH

brain's newest and often less efficient area: that "off-road" prefrontal cortex, or PFC.

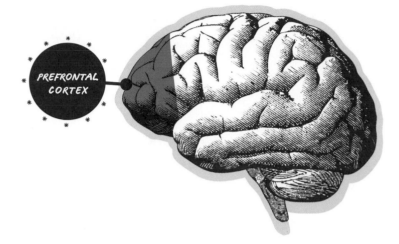

Of all of the brain's parts, the PFC is the least fuel-efficient. Which gives us a clue to why the brain tends to stay in that automatic mode. Science is still cracking the code on precisely how much extra juice the PFC demands, but we get a hint when we look at energy consumed by the brains of other primates. Whereas our furrier relatives tend to use around 10 percent of their energy to fuel their brains, we humans—the ones with the big PFCs—seem to use around twice that.

The PFC gets tired fast. If you've ever gone blank while solving a complicated problem, had your temper flare pointlessly when you were tired, or thought "My brain hurts" after an intense planning session, you've felt that depletion.

After all, in the world we evolved for, we needed our energy for things other than orchestrating long-term projects, staying sharp during a long day at the office, or navigating a world of constantly

Without STRUCTURE or DISCIPLINE, our thoughts run rampant on automatic. Because we have not learned how to more carefully MANAGE what goes on inside our brains, we remain vulnerable to not only what other people think about us, but also to advertising and/or political manipulation.

—JILL BOLTE TAYLOR, NEUROSCIENTIST, STROKE SURVIVOR, AUTHOR

buzzing distractions. Mostly, we worked on surviving, and surviving meant saving energy. The brain's first job was to keep us alive. Being prepared to fight with or run from whatever was lurking around the corner (or rustling in the grass) meant conserving energy. If a task wasn't geared for survival, our brains made sure there was some resistance to doing it.

Today, we often face decisions served better by thoughtful reflection than by lightning-fast reactions. Yet the resistance ingrained in our brains has not gone away.

However, if we're looking to bring more happiness into our lives, to align with purpose, or to feel more mastery and self-control, we need a different path. It involves the Watcher as well as an understanding of how today's reality can scramble our signals and leave us feeling less than happy—or in charge.

Understanding *that* means looking at what happiness actually is. It also means thinking about the things that lead to real happiness, the kind we all hunger for. Finding those things may mean disconnecting from some things we've assumed or simply done because they've become automatic habits. We've defaulted to them and forgotten to be watchful.

Routing our path to happiness means learning how, and when, to put our hands back on that metaphorical wheel. It means looking at routes that have become so familiar our automatic mode thinks they are *the* way, not merely *a* way. And it means investing the energy, and the practice, in activating parts of our brains that can fall out of use when we get too swept up in automatic mode— the brain's most powerful and efficient way of working.

It's easy to fall into automatic mode. We all do it. Yet learning to take back some control turns out to be a path to more happiness and satisfaction than we can find in the habitual paths. Even the work of taking the wheel, it turns out, helps us enjoy the road. And the practice of doing that helps boost the brain's capacity to do more of it. This is mindful work, the work of the Watcher—and something anyone can learn.

There are many ways to start activating this practice. One proven route hinges on something so basic to human nature that we often take it for granted or forget to actively nurture it. Especially in these busy, often distracting times, it's a time-honored benefit that often slips by the wayside. It's a simple thing, yet so core to our well-being and satisfaction that it's worth working to reclaim. It happens when we build connections.

Chemistry

MORE THAN A HUNDRED UNIQUE CHEMICALS FLOW THROUGH YOUR BRAIN AT ANY GIVEN TIME. THEIR LEVELS AND ACTIVITY ARE REGULATED BY A RANGE OF FACTORS: EVERYTHING FROM YOUR GENETICS TO WHAT'S HAPPENING IN YOUR ENVIRONMENT TO HOW YOU'VE LIVED YOUR LIFE SO FAR. HERE, MEET SOME OF THE MOST COMMON AND WELL-UNDERSTOOD BRAIN CHEMICALS—BOTH NEUROTRANSMITTERS AND HORMONES—AFFECTING HAPPINESS, HEALTH, AND SOCIAL INTERACTIONS.

∼∼ HAPPINESS MODULATORS ∼∼

DOPAMINE   **SEROTONIN**

DOPAMINE: *Ah, the thrill of the chase...the pursuit of a worthy goal...even the ping of an incoming "Like"! Meet dopamine: sparking feelings of enjoyment and gratification (as well as indulgence in guilty pleasures). This neurotransmitter boosts our happiness when we pursue or reach a goal...but can draw us in to too much of a good (or bad) thing.*

SEROTONIN: *There's nothing like the view from the top! Fulfillment, alignment with purpose, pride of long-term accomplishments: serotonin is the neurotransmitter often associated with self-esteem and life satisfaction. It helps you appreciate, enjoy, and reflect positively on the moments and achievements that have shaped the journey.*

~~~ STRESS MODULATORS ~~~

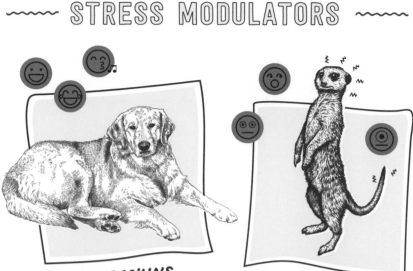

ENDORPHINS

CORTISOL

ENDORPHINS: *You can do it! Endorphins kick in when we're exercising, helping us power through resistance...or even pain. The runner's high, the athletic rush: they're what we get when these hormones are on the job. Good news: they also show up when we're laughing, and all-around help us feel more pleasure and less pain.*

CORTISOL: *Although normal levels help regulate our bodies, watch out: this hormone can build up with long-term stress and affect mental and physical health. Cortisol levels rise over time when we're chronically exposed to negative or threatening situations. Good news: healthy diet, exercise, rest, and mindfulness practices can all help to reduce cortisol levels.*

ADRENALINE: *Defend your turf or run like the wind! Excitement, arousal, danger: this hormone gets us up and moving...fast. Stressful situations fire it up as it prepares us for fight-or-flight. Adrenaline, also called epinephrine, shifts us into high gear in situations that are threatening, stressful, and/or physically exhilarating.*

ADRENALINE

～～ BONDING MODULATORS ～～

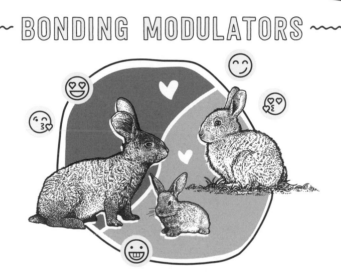

OXYTOCIN AND VASOPRESSIN

Bonding, caring, affection, connection: our "cuddle hormones" draw and keep us together. In women, oxytocin takes the lead in making the magic happen. For men, it's vasopressin. Either way, they help us feel the love...and keep the closeness coming. Aside from feeling nice, these hormones act as part of the glue of human connection. They help attract, draw, and keep us together.

Which Do You Choose?

EXPLORING THE TWO SIDES OF HAPPINESS

True happiness...is not attained through self-gratification but through fidelity to a worthy purpose.

—HELEN KELLER, AUTHOR, SPEAKER, GROUNDBREAKING ACTIVIST

What is happiness? It's a question many ask today, and they're not alone. Philosophers, pundits, and everyday people alike: we've grappled with this question since our earliest time.

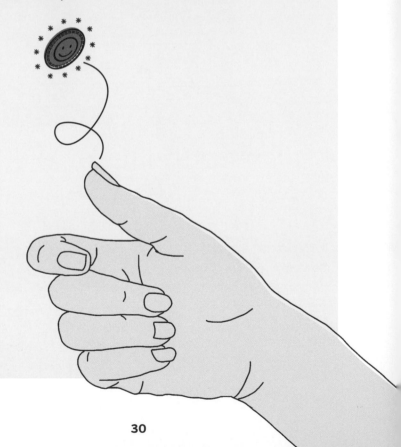

The Greeks puzzled over happiness for generations. Happiness, according to the philosopher Aristippus (c. 435–256 BCE), was pleasure—and as much of it as possible. Indulgence was the goal. Values, to him, had no real worth.

Aristippus's beliefs inspired the term "hedonic happiness," a label often given to impulsive and indulgent pleasures or the temporary relief of urges.

In contrast, "eudaimonic happiness," taught by Aristotle (384–322 BCE), elicited a deep well-being found in aligning with purpose, conquering obstacles, and achieving growth. This happiness grew from a virtuous life and the quest to actualize our potential. Tequila shots or video games wouldn't have made Aristotle's cut (if they'd been around in ancient Greece). Guilty pleasures and easy indulgences were not on the eudaimonic menu.

Aristippus and Aristotle may have lived before the dawn of cognitive neuroscience, but their thinking pointed to something we now know is true. Different feelings of happiness correlate to the presence of distinctly different brain chemicals.

Hedonic pleasures, generally, are the domain of dopamine: the chemical frequently associated with the chase of a desired object. Indulging urges, being distracted, or having "just one more" are generally dopamine-spiked behaviors that don't usually lead to lasting satisfaction.

Eudaimonic rewards, on the other hand, are linked to a different chemical: serotonin, which increases feelings of worthiness, belonging, and self-esteem. "To increase serotonin," says endurance athlete and author Christopher Bergland, "challenge yourself regularly and pursue things that reinforce purpose, meaning, and accomplishment. Being able to say 'I did it!' produces a feedback loop that reinforces confidence and creates an upward spiral of serotonin."

Both dopamine and serotonin help us feel pleasure and happiness. Yet for all of the good dopamine does—motivating us, helping us learn, literally getting us up and moving—it can wreak havoc on blood pressure, cause nervous tics, and elevate anxiety. It's associated with compulsive or addictive behaviors and can drive distraction, impulsivity, and lack of self-control.

Serotonin is different. Generally speaking, the body doesn't naturally produce too much of it. Having too little is a bigger issue: low levels of serotonin are associated with lethargy, binge eating, mood swings, and depression. So earning healthier happiness by choosing Aristotle's way over Aristippus's is good for your body as well as your brain.

Now, brain chemicals aren't bad or good. They're all necessary, and they each contribute to keeping our minds and bodies functioning.

But many casinos, advertisers, politicians, and even technology designers understand, or at least intuit, how these chemicals work—and use them to their advantage. Often, there's a deliberate plan to hook you on what they offer and keep you wanting more. Even without intent, anyone with an agenda can exploit the dark side of dopamine's power by activating your desires and promising you satisfaction through what they offer.

There's a big difference between the satisfaction Aristotle

encouraged and the indulgence Aristippus sought. Though they pondered happiness long ago, the questions they asked then remain at least as relevant today. What is the happiness we seek? What causes it, and why do we long for it? Above all, what are we willing to do to build that happiness?

And are we sure the happiness we're seeking is actually real satisfaction, rather than the easy tumble into distraction and indulgence dangled before us at every turn in the modern world?

Building
CONNECTIONS

We're taught that "alienation," when we withdraw or feel alone, is a craving for something sexual, material, or physical...when in truth, it's the circuitry within our souls and minds hinting to be connected outside of our TVs and computer monitors. What many of us mistake for depression is actually a need to be understood, or to see desires come to fruition.

—SUZY KASSEM, AUTHOR, ARTIST

LOOKING AT THE TECHNOLOGY and data, you might assume we all feel more connected to each other than ever.

After all, billions of us log in to Facebook every day. We search Google 2.5 billion times and send more than 6 billion text messages every twenty-four hours. And the count is rising.

On Snapchat, we share 9,000 snaps per *second*.

Yet other data—about people, not technology—tells a different story.

One out of four Americans reports struggling with loneliness. One in five finds it persistent. Depression is on the rise as a global health risk, predicted to be the world's second most prevalent medical condition (heart disease is number one) by 2020. And depression, research shows, is often a disease of loneliness.

We may be connected, technically speaking. But our digital connections don't necessarily leave us feeling that way. In fact, they might be making us feel more alone. And feeling connected, with real people, is at the very core of our ability to be happy.

Interaction vs. Transaction

Access to technology has brought us all kinds of efficiencies that make life easier, smoother, and more predictable. We rely on our tech to help us do more faster and to automate an increasing number of everyday processes.

Efficiencies are great. But they're not why we're here. Our lives mean more than simply saving time so we can get more done. Satisfaction doesn't grow from doing more stuff, some of it meaningless, faster and faster.

And all that time we spend staring at screens—half of our waking hours for the average American—is time we *don't* spend on things that can make us happier.

Screens don't lead us to happiness. Our brains know it, and our hearts feel it. Stress levels climb, year over year, yet nobody knows how to break the cycle.

Our bodies know it too. Loneliness hurts, and that's more than a metaphor. UCLA psychologist Naomi Eisenberger studied how feelings of loneliness and exclusion triggered activity in some of the brain regions associated with senses of physical pain. Social pain, her research showed, could hurt so much people *physically* felt it.

We're here to interact, not simply to transact. On some level, we seem to know this. But distractions from tech and other temptations promise easy answers and quick fixes only a click away, so we keep clicking.

Happiness for an hour: take a nap.
Happiness for a day: go fishing.
Happiness for a year: inherit a fortune.
Happiness for a lifetime? Help someone else.
—CHINESE PROVERB

Messages all around us try to convince us that happiness is simply one more purchase, night on the town, or date away. Even as FOMO (fear of missing out) rivets us to our devices, calling us to document rather than enjoy the moment (in hopes of winning flurries of "likes"), many of us feel more and more alone. The very action of capturing and sharing our moments directs us toward our tech and away from the only lasting source of happiness: the real world and the people around us.

Not convinced? Multiple studies show that when we snap a quick picture, we barely retain the memory of what the camera saw. The brain seems to decide we've outsourced that memory, so it doesn't bother to map it. We capture it. Yet we don't retain it.

Social platforms put us in the shallows, so to speak, of interaction. A quick "like" or "sad face" may signal engagement to the person on the other side of the post and release a quick chemical that may feel like happiness, but it's fleeting. Our retention of what we liked or were sad about on social platforms doesn't last. Nor does it really connect us to people. We've all seen posts on social media about friends' losses or heartbreaks. Yet we may not recall the loss when we encounter that friend in real life.

As we tune in to our tech instead of to each other, we pay a price.

It is not the forces of darkness but of shallowness that everywhere threaten the **TRUE**, and the **GOOD**, and the **BEAUTIFUL**, and that ironically address themselves as deep and profound. It is an exuberant and fearless shallowness that everywhere is the modern danger, and that everywhere nonetheless calls to us as savior.

—KEN WILBUR, PSYCHOLOGIST, SCHOLAR, AUTHOR

Connecting IRL

Connecting IRL (in real life) is no longer the simple, natural action it once was. Even in the real world, we disconnect. Scan the line at your favorite coffee shop and see how many people are looking at their phones, not at each other. How many stay glued to them even as they place their order and leave the counter without saying "hello" or "thank you" to the person who took their order? We may think this doesn't matter: that small, casual interactions don't register in the brain as connection. But they do.

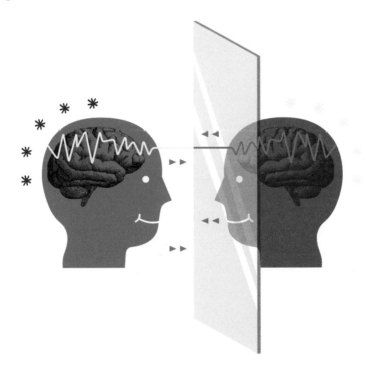

A smile activates mirror neurons—special signals that fire when we act and when we observe others acting—making grins literally contagious. Smiles are like parties for the brain. They activate neuropeptides that work to reduce stress and spread happy messages throughout the body. Dopamine, serotonin, and endorphins also fire up, triggering relaxation and lowering blood pressure. Sensations of pain may ease, thanks to endorphins. Both the smiler and the "smilee" usually feel a mood boost.

We shall never know all the good a simple SMILE can do.

—MOTHER TERESA

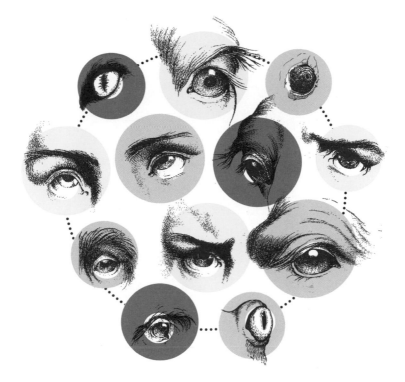

Friendly eye contact works even better. Human eyes are unique: our pupils are surrounded by white, and the shape of our eye opening makes sure the white is visible. Why? Anthropologists propose that our more-open eyes helped us know who to trust and cooperate with. Most primate babies watch the head direction of the grown-up primates they're learning from. But human babies do something different: they watch eyes.

In fact, a Purdue University study found that eye contact, even short glances between strangers, sparked a feeling of connection that wasn't experienced when subjects looked the other way. In their research, people who didn't receive eye contact, even in casual settings, reported feeling ignored and unseen, a feeling that hurt.

The only reason we don't open our hearts and minds to other people is that they trigger confusion in us that we don't feel BRAVE enough or sane enough to deal with. To the degree that we look clearly and compassionately at ourselves, we feel CONFIDENT and FEARLESS about looking into someone else's eyes.

—PEMA CHÖDRÖN, BUDDHIST NUN, AUTHOR

Think about that chain reaction as you look to that coffee shop line.

Connection as a Survival Mechanism

Neuroscientist and social psychologist John Cacioppo has dedicated his career to understanding loneliness and its effect on the brain and body. "The absence of social connection triggers the same primal alarm bells as hunger, thirst, and physical pain," he explains. "Loneliness puts your brain into self-preservation mode... The visual cortex becomes more active while the area responsible for empathy becomes less active."

In self-preservation mode, higher-level thinking becomes more elusive. We lock into default patterns, making it harder to access the Watcher or the functions of the PFC. The brain handles social threat and physical threat in similar ways, firing the fight-or-flight response, which reduces blood supply to the PFC and even, through the adrenal system, to our vital organs.

There is a word in South Africa—UBUNTU—a word that captures Mandela's greatest gift: his recognition that we are all bound together in ways that are invisible to the eye; that there is a oneness to humanity; that we achieve ourselves by sharing ourselves with others and caring for those around us.

—PRESIDENT BARACK OBAMA, SPEAKING AT THE MEMORIAL SERVICE FOR NELSON MANDELA

We feel it. When we feel shunned in a social setting, our caution grows. The brain locks in to subconscious or unconscious patterns, searching for what has worked before. Maybe we reach for another drink or chomp a bite of something we don't really want. We feel diminished, even confused.

As we grab the drink and grease-burger and head for the more predictable reward system of our apps, email, or TV, we pay a price. Dr. Cacioppo's work shows that loneliness is even riskier than obesity in some age groups. Social isolation is correlated to a 20 percent increase in mortality rates relative to "not lonely" research groups. As we continue to direct our attention to things rather than to people, our brains adapt and rewire, making this shift the new normal. But this normal isn't leading us to happiness. It can leave us feeling lost, out of sorts, and alone.

Timeless Wisdom

"I see you" is a traditional greeting used in some southern African cultures. Sometimes another phrase, "I am here to be seen," completes the greeting, creating a circle of acknowledgment. You can almost feel the mirror neurons firing.

These respectful, socially connecting words likely rose into custom as a declaration of good intent. But they signal something core to human happiness: our need to connect with each other. "I see you" hints at the African concept of *Ubuntu*, which tells us that "A person is a person through other people."

Our brains would agree.

How often do we feel ignored? How many people do we pass each day whom we never notice or acknowledge? How many more if we're tuned to our cell phones? Do we really "see" others when we tap "like" on a social post?

When digital transactions serve as proxy for real-life interactions, we feel invisible and excluded. A deeper sort of FOMO can kick in.

Fortunately, there's another path, one that helps fire our brain's reward chemicals and wire new maps to happier patterns. Neuroplasticity—the brain's ability to update itself by mapping new neural connections—gives us the power to reclaim pathways we've unintentionally lost and build new ones. But we have to get out of automatic mode. It takes intention—and practice.

Yet as the brain fires, so it wires. Which gives you a good reason to start doing more of whatever it is you really want to do, especially if that means reconnecting with people.

Here are some ways to get started.

Disconnect to Reconnect

If feeling more connected sounds good to you, try these simple steps.

LOOK UP FROM THE TECH

Choose one real-world thing you'd like to do more of and one screen-based thing you'd like to do less of. Jot your intentions down, and put them somewhere visible, where you see them every day. Celebrate your progress, and start again if you lapse.

Building or breaking habits takes work. But learning, it turns out, activates parts of your brain that contribute to feelings of well-being and mastery. What's more, integration of new information or actions often take place in the PFC, revving up parts of the brain that help us build willpower, make satisfying decisions, and mindfully navigate what's going on around us.

The best place to meet people? Easy: anywhere your TV is not.

START SMALL

The brain maps familiar thoughts and actions with ever-increasing efficiency. For better or worse, these maps make it easy to see and do things the way we have in the past. We become blind to these assumptions: they become automatic. Changing them takes work and repetition. So even small changes can start out slowly.

To reduce resistance, work *with* your brain. Associate new patterns with familiar actions. This helps your brain build new actions on existing maps. Slip your phone into your pocket as you walk toward the coffee shop. Remind yourself to say good morning before you place your order. Watch what happens.

Want positive reinforcement? Try smiling. As your mirror neurons fire when that barista smiles back, your brain will update its maps and prime itself for smiling more, with increasingly less effort.

SMILE...it makes people wonder what you're up to.

—UNKNOWN

VOLUNTEER

Every community, every destination, every affinity group likely needs more help than they are getting. What do you believe in? Who or what do you want to support? Getting hands-on with something that makes a difference is a surefire way to experience a brain-nourishing (and heart-filling) form of satisfaction. And it's a great way to connect with others. You're likely to find kindred spirits—and the deep satisfaction of contributing toward a shared goal.

Be a RAINBOW in someone else's cloud.

—MAYA ANGELOU, AUTHOR AND PRESIDENTIAL INAUGURAL POET

RETHINK SOLITUDE

"Loneliness," said theologian Paul Tillich, "expresses the pain of being alone, and solitude expresses the glory."

Sometimes what seems to be loneliness can actually be a sense of disconnection from purpose. Yes, we all need and deserve social connection. But we also desire and deserve a feeling that we're making a difference in the world: that our contributions matter.

You matter. As do your contributions, whatever they may be. Yet our sense of purpose can get sucked into the vortex of everyday reality, with its unending to-do lists, commutes, and pressures.

We come home feeling worn and depleted. Understandably, we crave the low-resistance stuff. But too much vegging out can eat into happiness. The typical triggers and rewards of apps or video games, TV series, or even our inboxes activate brain chemicals that can increase our sense of stress, isolation, and threat. When we feel those, we're less open to social engagement. We shut down and stay in, which weakens the maps that show us how to open back up again.

How can we reverse the cycle and turn alone time into satisfying time?

Self-care is one place to begin. Even small things that take care of *you* are a surefire way to find strength in solitude. Cooking well for yourself, even once a week, or perfecting a yoga sun salutation…each small step can help you and your body find a bit of glory. Since the brain wires what it fires, you'll also get a boost that helps point you toward the next healthy step.

Since we know dopamine cues motivation and progress toward rewards, we can use that knowledge to boost our healthy drives. If your homeward commute is usually filled with dreams of vegging out, visualize yourself drawing in your sketchbook or practicing that new guitar chord instead. Invite the Watcher to help, helping your brain prime itself for your desired activity. Not convinced? Consider this: competitive athletes use similar brain exercises as they train and prepare to compete. If it's good enough for them, you deserve it too.

BE PATIENT

Somewhere inside, we know connections are key to happiness. In a way, feelings of loneliness or isolation are like a signal telling us we want something other than what we have. Yet, ironically, feelings of loneliness can actually make us more self-protective. When we feel threatened, it's true: we tend to shut down.

That's how our brains work, for all sorts of complicated reasons. Yet we're conditioned to blame ourselves, to think it's a problem with *us*. Sadly, the more we think this, the more our responses can lock the loneliness in.

Sometimes even our best attempts don't go as we planned. We may be friendlier in the outside world or make efforts to mingle with new people, but the "tribe finding" doesn't go as we'd hoped.

That can be hard. But try to remember that everyone's experiencing the stress and distraction of everyday life. Even with the

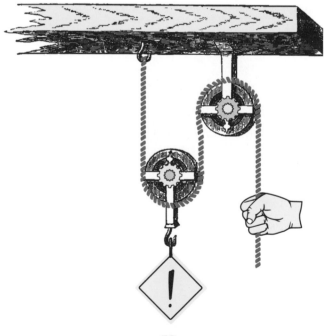

help of mirror neurons, some people may not be ready to respond to friendly overtures.

If this happens, look at it as resistance training for your brain. If you get a negative response, let it go. Don't mirror their lead. Use your PFC to sense that something must be hard for them (empathy is a core strength of the PFC, and the more you use it, the more resilient you get). Maybe wish them, sincerely, an especially good day, even if you only wish it from afar. Who knows? You may be helping them. You'll definitely be helping yourself.

But one thing is clear. Turning to our tech is doing more than turning us away from more satisfying connections. It's wiring our brains to expect more predictable, linear, cause-and-effect transactions than real life in all its nonlinear joy. This can leave us feeling impatient and intolerant when we interact with others and interact authentically, which in turn fuels the cycles of loneliness.

If we want change, we need to master ourselves. That starts with mastering the things that keep us from connecting, whether they're our all-too-available distractions or routine habits that separate us from each other. There's an easy way to turn the tide. It starts when we unplug.

The Harvard Happiness Study
LESSONS ACROSS LIFETIMES POINT TO ONE CONSISTENT THEME

*Friendship is born at that moment when
one person says to another: "What! You
too? I thought I was the only one."*

—C. S. LEWIS, WRITER

Way back in 1938, when a group of researchers asked "What makes for a good life?" they didn't know what they would learn. But they were willing to wait a long time for an answer. After watching 724 people for more than seventy-five years, they found one—something we all can learn from.

The lives and fates of these 724 people, all Harvard graduates, were as individual as they were. Some lived in urban settings, some in rural. Their professions, financial success, activities, and health varied widely. Some weathered failure and loss. Some battled medical challenges. Some succeeded in their careers; some did not. One (John F. Kennedy) became a president.

And some became happier than others. Across the many interviews and checkpoints that tracked these lives, those that found the most happiness credited one simple thing.

Connection.

Those who looked back on their lives with the greatest satisfaction were those who felt most connected to people they loved.

"People who are more socially connected to family, friends, or community are happier, physically healthier, and longer-lived than others," the study revealed. "People who are more isolated than they want to be find they are less happy. Health and brain functioning decline sooner. They live shorter lives than people who feel connected."

If the pull of distractions and devices is disconnecting us from family or social circles, or even making it only a little bit easier to withdraw from checking in with a friend or greeting a neighbor, are we fueling scenarios that reduce our happiness? In fairness, the Harvard study emphasized the impact of deep, close relationships, not things like simple hellos or greetings to people we barely know.

But even casual exchanges spark healthy activity in our brains. Kindness or helpful acts may seem like things we do for others—but they also help us. Opening a door for a stranger or picking up a dropped glove—even smiling in the coffee line—can activate the chemical responses that leave us feeling uplifted and balanced. Better yet is when we share our attention with people close to us or engage in real conversation with others in our social circles. Even small steps toward truly seeing those around us can boost healthier brain activity, and (since what fires, wires) make it easier for us to take more little steps, and then bigger ones, that build our sense of connection.

Think of one person in your world you've been meaning to connect with: to get to know better or to actually make time for. Surprise them: write them a note, find time to talk, or tell them about something that made you think of them. Ask them about something they enjoy, and find out why they like it. Tell them something nice you remember about them. Better yet, find something to do together that you'll both remember.

You'll not only be building your bond. You'll be improving your brain—and theirs too—while creating moments that add to the scenery on your lifelong path to happiness.

Unplugging

We use our gadgets for distraction and enter-
tainment. We use them to avoid work while
giving the impression that we're actually
working hard.

—MEGHAN DAUM, AUTHOR, COLUMNIST

ATA CONFIRMS WHAT WE have all noticed: all this tech we're using isn't delivering the ease and happiness it's advertised to promise. According to a global World Economic Forum study:

DIGITAL MEDIA USERS OFTEN SPEND MORE HOURS ONLINE THAN THEY SLEEP, YET ONLY 50 PERCENT BELIEVE IT IMPROVES QUALITY OF LIFE.

FIVE OUT OF SIX TECH USERS SAID THEY WEREN'T SURE DIGITAL CONSUMPTION HAD A POSITIVE EFFECT ON THEIR LIVES.

PARTICIPANTS' SOCIAL MEDIA USE ALONE CONSUMED AN AVERAGE OF 1.8 HOURS (30 PERCENT OF TOTAL DAILY ONLINE TIME) PER DAY.

That same study confirmed that social skills and empathy shifted downward as people spent more time online. Stress, vulnerability to addictive behavior, and a decline in physical activity also correlated to increases in screen time.

Facts from Digital Detox, a community dedicated to helping people use tech more mindfully, drive the point home:

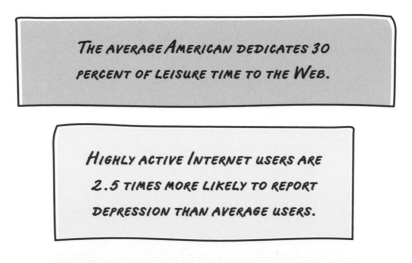

THE AVERAGE AMERICAN DEDICATES 30 PERCENT OF LEISURE TIME TO THE WEB.

HIGHLY ACTIVE INTERNET USERS ARE 2.5 TIMES MORE LIKELY TO REPORT DEPRESSION THAN AVERAGE USERS.

33 PERCENT OF PEOPLE ADMIT TO HIDING FROM FAMILY AND FRIENDS TO CHECK SOCIAL MEDIA.

95 PERCENT OF PEOPLE USE SOME TYPE OF ELECTRONICS IN THE HOUR LEADING UP TO BED.

UNPLUGGING FROM TECH FOR JUST ONE DAY CAN GIVE SOME PEOPLE MENTAL AND PHYSICAL WITHDRAWAL SYMPTOMS.

Rising Challenges

Psychological disorders that didn't even exist a few years ago—Internet addiction and video gaming disorder, to name two—are now medically diagnosable. Dedicated residential treatment centers have popped up to help people recover from these dependencies. A growing community called Tech Addiction Anonymous offers twelve-step support to help people break free and stay clean.

And while research indicates that excessive use of digital media can negatively influence cognitive functions, behavioral development, and even mental and physical health, we keep plugging in.

We see the signs everywhere. Distracted walking accidents injure more than ten thousand people each year. In a Swedish study, heavy tech use among young adults was correlated to less sleep, more stress, and a decline in mental health. Researchers in London found that interruptions from phone calls, texts, and email at work lowered IQs as significantly as a marijuana high or a night without sleep.

Yet multiple studies confirm a consistent truth: that the average American spends more than *half* of his or her waking life staring at a screen.

Tech is changing our lives powerfully, fast, and in ways we didn't anticipate. And anything changing our lives is also changing our brains.

In the language of tech itself, we're being hacked.

This increasing reliance isn't adding to our happiness. In fact, as the World Economic Forum study showed, it may be interfering with it. Our emphasis on efficiency, largely ushered in by tech, often puts us in the smile-free zone, multitasking one thing off of our list so we can get on to the next.

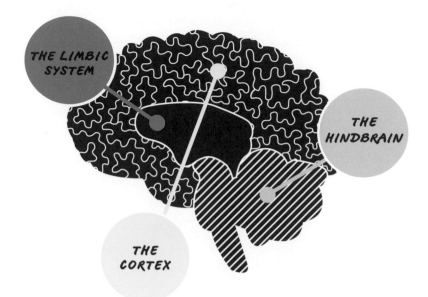

It's ironic that tech's promise of more productivity, and even more connection, once meant more time for the people and things we love. In reality, our easy, always-on connectedness can pull us away from real productivity and certainly from people and things that matter. Many of us are left feeling we have less time, and we need every moment simply to keep up.

Now, to be fair, there's a counterpoint to any opinion or research. For every study on how tech is limiting our happiness, another shows the opposite. Examples abound of people who've found long-lost friends, built supportive communities, and faced major hardships with the help of tech.

And logically, we know tech helps us in countless ways. It can keep us connected to faraway loved ones in ways no letter or phone call could. And it can tie us to communities of support and affinity when we face hardship or build change. And it can certainly help us create, design, and share work that matters deeply to us. There are plenty of benefits to be found in tech. But every choice comes with a trade-off, as many of us feel inside.

Take what you wish...
AND PAY FOR IT.
—SPANISH PROVERB

Attention Deficits

If we'd known the price we'd pay for that first seductive swipe of our finger across a glassy screen, we might have done a few things differently. In an alternate reality with full understanding, we might have taken a more measured, intentional approach to the way we let tech into our lives—and we might be feeling more calm, purposeful, connected, and in control than we do today.

"Most people," asserts author and teacher Darius Foroux, "don't use technology but are rather used *by* it.

"Apps, games, videos, articles, commercials, TV shows, are all designed to keep your attention," he continues. "So without you knowing it, you waste countless hours every week. Your attention is all over the place, but not at the right place."

To be EVERYWHERE is to be NOWHERE.

— SENECA

The brain's incredible plasticity—its ability to wire what it fires—lets it adapt to the changes we put it through in near real time, updating its maps to our reality and converting new actions to routine, unseen defaults.

But the amount of time we spend on tech, and the way it interacts with our brains' cognitive and reward systems, are a far cry from what our brains evolved for. Biologically speaking, our brains didn't see this one coming.

Somewhere inside, something feels off. "I didn't think it would be this way," a quiet voice might seem to say.

Maybe you have felt your tech was in charge of you rather than you in charge of it.

Maybe you've ended a day wondering what you actually did with your day.

Maybe you've let a guilty pleasure take over and then faced the struggle of catching up with the "real" stuff the morning after.

Maybe you, like so many of us, have walked away from time with a friend and realized neither of you were really present, actually paying attention, as you spoke.

Maybe you've even felt that way with a loved one at home.

You're not alone. We're all feeling it. And unfortunately, it's not getting better.

Changing the Path

Distractions have always been part of human life. In fact, distractibility can help us. In our early human days, our response to distraction might have made our day or saved our life. Looking away from the task at hand let us spot opportunities, perhaps catching the sparkle of a rare stone on the path ahead. Maybe it helped us enjoy, even share, special moments, as when a colorful bird flitted close by. It certainly saved us from danger when a rustle in the grass put us on high alert, fight-or-flight response ready.

Distractibility is part of life, helpful for survival, and one of the ways we have fun. A little break can soothe the brain, refresh us, and bring serendipity as things happen around us.

But we seem to be dealing with too much of a good thing. And nothing in our human history has prepared us—or our brains—for the carefully designed "lure 'em in!" hooks built into the tech we choose and use.

Getting Hacked

Always-on distractions and interruptions are changing our brains, and not in ways that build mastery and satisfaction. And as Darius Foroux suggests, it's happening by design. Books and workshops coach user experience designers to understand the brain—the better to guide the trigger-and-reward responses behind conversation, sharing, likes, loves, retweets, reloads, upgrades, and OMGs.

These are the rewards *they're* after, and they have the science to get what they want. Our brains, in a way, have been blindsided by their skill. What starts as a fun diversion can shift as the brain reacts and rewires to dopamine hooks…and then to the next one, leaving us craving "more, more, more!"

Distraction is no path to satisfaction or mastery. Too much of anything good—be it chocolate or our favorite movie or a diet of pleasurable moments—gets less good pretty fast.

"It's sucking away our quality of life," claims author and NYU professor Jonathan Safran Foer. "The more distracted we become, and the more emphasis we place on speed at the expense of depth… the less likely and able we are to care… I've found myself checking email while giving my kids a bath, jumping to the Internet when a sentence or idea doesn't come effortlessly in my writing, searching for shade on a beautiful day so I can see the screen of my phone.

"Sometimes we look to tech for the easy answers—which may

not really be what we want. We've gotten used to on-demand information. But are we sure those easy answers deliver happiness?

"We consumers forget," he continues, "that technology always...produces certain affects... But successful companies do not. They remember and profit enormously. We forget at the expense of who we are."

Our easy, endless access keeps us clicking and liking or watching "just one more" episode. Like a tequila shot, the fleeting pleasure these actions deliver may not give us anything we actually want. What seems like a good idea at the time doesn't necessarily translate into real happiness.

Hacking Back

Distraction, especially as delivered through tech's precisely engineered experiences, can hack the way our brains work. But by understanding and working with our brains, we have ways to hack back.

It takes effort and intention: the work of the Watcher. It doesn't mean abandoning tech or winding back the clock to simpler times. We wouldn't do that even if we could.

Yet by understanding the most powerful device in the world, that three-pound marvel we carry with us everywhere, we can decide—even direct—what we really want.

If quick-fix enjoyment isn't giving you what you're after, if you're craving a sense of mastery in the way you work, or if a call to a deeper purpose draws you, congratulations. You're ready to unplug, at least some of the time. You can start practicing ways to lean and wean away from outside lures and automatic responses.

My wife and I debated learning the sex of our first child before birth. I raised the issue with my uncle, a gynecologist who had delivered more than five thousand babies. He said, "If a doctor looks at a screen and tells you, you will have information. If you find out at the moment of birth, you will have a MIRACLE."

I don't believe in miracles, but [we] followed his advice...and HE WAS RIGHT.

—JONATHAN SAFRAN FOER,
AUTHOR AND PROFESSOR

Focus and mastery are what you'll earn in return. You may gain more sense of purpose. You may come to love the peace of quiet downtime, uninterrupted, on your own terms. You may find new enjoyments, new connections, or new practices that bring you real satisfaction.

Or you may simply come back to where you are now, but with more mindfulness and clarity.

Getting back in charge is a big change for many of us. To achieve it, we may need a boost. Good news: that boost is waiting for you in the next pages as you learn to master your mind.

Mastering
YOUR MIND

"Be careful what you water your dreams with. Water them with worry and fear and you will produce weeds that choke the life from your dream. Water them with optimism and solutions and you will cultivate success. Always be on the lookout for ways to turn a problem into an opportunity for success. Always be on the lookout for ways to nurture your dream."

—LAO TZU, CHINESE SAGE, PHILOSOPHER

MASTERING YOUR MIND IS about focus. It's about clearing away the noise and working with your brain to move through challenges and resistance.

Focused work, compared to distraction? Well, it's like the difference between a deep-tissue massage and a pat on the back.

Both have their place. But no number of pats can ever create that "Aaaaah" we feel when firm pressure meets tight muscle and melts the tension away.

Yet deep work takes *work*. We resist it, and a brain accustomed to distraction struggles with it even more.

That brain messes with our minds. We tend to see successful people as lucky, or gifted, or simply born in the right place at the right time. Sure, external factors influence every fate. The right environments, teachers, or opportunities certainly favor some people to succeed.

But more often it's about *practice*: focus, diligence, and commitment. Growth. Resilience. And overcoming the all-too-available distractions that trick us away from our goals.

"Luck?" answered tennis star Serena Williams when asked about her unrivaled career. "Luck has nothing to do with it, because I have spent many, many hours, countless hours, on the court working for my one moment in time, not knowing when it would come."

There's real truth in her statement. If happiness is about satisfaction, how do we know when—or how—we'll reach the goals we're working on? What if we don't? What if someone beats us to it, or the rules change right before we win the game?

Maybe it's not worth trying, our unconscious or subconscious self might tell us. It didn't work before. Why would it work now?

There's a reason we *pay* attention. TIME and FOCUS are our most precious currency.

—UNKNOWN

That invisible or routine mode is right: we don't always know how hard work will pay off. We question whether the long-term rewards will be worth the short-term trade-offs. Maybe that's why we're so ready to give our attention away when a distraction comes along.

Yet you probably already know—even *feel*, in some hard-to-explain way—that no number of small, shallow tasks can deliver the satisfaction we get when we accomplish things that matter. Saying "email" or "nothing" when someone asks "What did you do today?" doesn't satisfy us *or* our brain's hunger for meaningful work.

Yet email, or a long list of distractions that add up to nothing, *can* fill our time, masquerading as (or even becoming) our daily work.

We want *more*: something deeper, something that feels uniquely ours, something with purpose. Something that leads to satisfaction and mastery, to deeper forms of happiness.

The good news is we can find it. We may need to learn some new practices and leave some old ones behind. Like anything worthy, it takes work.

How to L*E*A*R*N*
BUILDING NEW HABITS ON EXISTING BRAIN MAPS

Wealth, if you use it, comes to an end.
Learning, if you use it, increases.
—SWAHILI PROVERB

To pay attention, this is our ENDLESS and proper WORK.

—MARY OLIVER, POET

From our curious childhoods to the night-before-finals crams of our school days to the "Where are those keys?" panics of our adult lives, our brains process information in ever-changing ways.

Some ways work better than others. Try this: Which do you remember better? The first time you played in snow? Or the details of a key religious milestone from the 1500s you memorized in college?

If you're like most people, you probably answered "snow." If you actually remembered an event (and you aren't a history buff), maybe you remembered the Diet of Worms, whose odd-but-real name describes a historic assembly of the Holy Roman Empire back in 1521.

If you did remember that name, it probably wasn't the content that you recalled. It was the strange name, which likely stood out in that history class as a daydream interrupter, mapping itself to your existing mental maps of humor, oddities, and "invertebrates that squirm." And, *voilà*, all these years later, the Diet of Worms pops up.

Perhaps not a good visual, but an illustration of how true learning occurs.

Learning builds upon learning throughout our lives. And multisensory moments map themselves to a wider array of maps. This is especially true in childhood. Imagine your first experience of snow. The surprising crunch of a freezing white substance, the sight of little flakes floating down from the sky, the soft tickle of cold on our cheeks, maybe even the challenge of waddling in a hand-me-down parka and too-big boots: new experiences etch vivid images in our young brains. They also form a foundation for future memories that will map upon them.

Memory champions use multisensory associations to bolster their maps. When scientists scanned the brains of professional memorizers (really, such a thing exists) while they were ingraining new information, they saw something different than what they saw in ordinary folks.

"Memory champions lit up different parts of their brains," explains Joshua Foer, a memory expert. "They used, or seemed to use, parts of the brain involved in spatial memory and navigation."

Foer uses the timeless "Memory Palace" technique to master his retention. He actively associates visual images, bawdy humor, current events, and movement to rapidly connect new thoughts to as many existing maps as possible. He "recruits," so to speak, from sensory and experiential processing centers to anchor the thoughts he seeks to memorize.

We can use this thinking to improve our own retention. If we want to ingrain information, habits, attitudes, or anything new, we can work with our brains to help them absorb and encode more efficiently.

Here's how.

1 LABEL: Name what you want your brain to do. "Let's learn this new habit," or "Tonight, we'll master three conjugations." This primes your brain's attention and directs it toward a task. It also prepares it to connect with existing knowledge or action maps. Labels warm your brain up and prepare it to fire, so it's ready to wire.

2 ENCOURAGE: Imagine a positive result your new habit or knowledge will lead to, then talk about it in positive terms.

Visualize it: top athletes do this as they train to reach audacious goals. Coach yourself toward that goal the way you would a close friend. And give yourself credit as you get a bit closer to it every day. Want to take this to the next level? Invite the Watcher to join in. Having that higher self reinforce the encouragement increases your brain's sense of the experience. It may even add to maps in your PFC if you associate your progress with higher-order, mindful goals you're working on.

3 **ASSOCIATE:** Build mental bridges between new information or activity and maps your brain has already established. If it's a new habit, do what Stanford behavioral researcher B. J. Fogg recommends: start small, and bridge the new thing to something you already do. Want to get more organized? Jot down daily priorities after you press "brew" on your coffee maker. Want to break the unending tech habit? Shut down your laptop before you floss at night.

Once your new tiny habits are established, you can add to them, building new maps step-by-step until you have a whole new habit.

If it's new knowledge you're after, take a page from Foer's memory book. Associate the thought with visual images or recruit from other brain centers. Moving while visualizing, coming up with rhymes (we can all still sing the alphabet song, right?), or identifying related memories and intentionally connecting the dots: each of these strengthens the maps between established knowledge and new learning.

4 **REPEAT:** Repetition speeds learning. In fact, it can even convince our brains to replace known facts with known falsehoods (the "illusory fact effect"). If you want to learn faster, extend repetition across different modes. Take what you want to learn, and write it down. Narrate it to a friend, to yourself, even to your dog. Sing about it. Put a reminder in a place you visit every day. If you slip or skip, don't worry. Start again, and your brain will bridge back to the maps you've started and continue building. Stick with it. Repetition is the glue.

5 **NIGHTTIME:** Your brain prunes while you're sleeping. It preserves information you're actively using and tends to let go—slowly but surely—of the stuff you're not.

If you want to retain something, make sure it doesn't get pruned at night. Bring it to mind as part of your evening routine. Visualize it as you prepare for sleep. If other thoughts come up, replace them with the things you want to remember. Try using your final moments of wakefulness to remember three things: your main goal for the next day, a longer-term plan you're working on, and what you appreciated most about your day. These thoughts can override the usual nighttime brain chatter. They bring a sense of peace and purpose. And they may be waiting for you the next morning, priming you to focus on what matters and anticipate what you'll appreciate most in the day ahead.

Learning is one of those brain activities that sparks a range of happy chemicals. But it can also cause stress. Remember to be patient with yourself as you convert "new" into "familiar and easy." Stress chemicals like cortisol can limit activity in certain brain areas, reducing the use of multisensory maps. So be a friend to yourself, like a helpful coach. Invite the Watcher in to join the pep talk. With time and commitment, not only will you have mastered what you wanted to learn, you'll also have built a new map for how to L*E*A*R*N* the next thing.

Focus

We humans are problem solvers. We (and our brains) evolved by using our intelligence to survive in the world around us. We learned to follow tracks and weave grass into useful baskets. We perfected healing remedies and gained year-over-year knowledge from the seasons and stars.

Focus and diligent work shaped our early brains. It took time, care, and practiced technique to make a perfect arrowhead or to know which leaves cured a headache (or made things worse).

Of course, there was always the capacity for distraction: we needed that too. Our survival depended on noticing a rustle in the grass. Our social order blossomed as we made time for rituals or laughed when the village goof-off cartwheeled across our path.

We weren't optimized, though, for a barrage of small, light activities or for hopping between different modes like a frog jumping across a pond. Happiness—the kind we want—isn't "hoppiness." It comes from satisfaction, and for that, we have to work.

We probably wouldn't have survived if our ancestors had faced the onslaught of distractions we face today. Want proof? If modern pedestrians don't notice a giant Wookiee waving at them as they text their way down the street, it's a good guess our ancient predecessors, if they'd been clicking and tapping away, wouldn't have noticed a saber-toothed tiger. The rest, as they say, would have been history.

Deep Work

Studying, completing big projects, staying patient with long-term goals, even going out and weeding the garden: we "want" to do them, "wish" we could do them, or feel like we "should" do them.

But we find easy ways to blow them off.

Do we feel happy afterward? No. We may have enjoyed a guilty pleasure, but the memory of what we should have done nags at us. And reality is still waiting when the party's over.

GET REAL ABOUT THE TRADE-OFFS

Think about *why* you're doing the things that distract you and soak up your time. How do they serve you? How do the results justify the price you paid?

"We are only beginning to get our minds around the costs" of constant distraction, says publishing heavyweight Andrew Sullivan, "if we are even prepared to accept that there *are* costs." In his article "I Used to Be a Human Being," he warns, "An endless bombardment of news, gossip, and images has rendered us manic information addicts. It broke me. It might break you, too."

Knowing *why* you're doing something is a big step toward deciding *what* you want to do and *how*. Once you realize how routine habits or thoughts are interfering with the things you really want to master, you can start mapping your path away from the old and toward the new.

HARNESS YOUR REWARD SYSTEM

If dopamine motivates us to pursue goals and serotonin rewards us for achieving them, why not fire both of them up?

Visualizing the path to (and results of) deep work might help. After all, it does for athletes. Early in their training, they're coached (and self-coached) to see themselves as champions. In their mind's eye, they envision the practices as well as the various challenges and victories that lead to success. As they approach the starting block, they use their mind to foresee each step ahead.

You can do this too. As you prepare for deep work, break your steps down. Visualize them. What will that résumé showcase when it's ready for review? What will the garage look like when it's finally empty? Visualizing primes our brains to fire up reward chemicals, making the lure of lesser rewards (like the usual distractions) a whole lot less interesting.

Identify the core factors that determine SUCCESS and HAPPINESS in your professional and personal life. Adopt a tool only if its POSITIVE IMPACTS on these factors substantially outweigh its negative impacts.

—CAL NEWPORT, GEORGETOWN PROFESSOR, STUDY HACKER, DEEP WORK EVANGELIST

I AM THE GREATEST.
I said that even before
I knew I was.

**—MUHAMMAD ALI, PRIZEFIGHTER,
G.O.A.T. (GREATEST OF ALL TIME)**

DECIDE WHAT YOU *CARE* ABOUT

Perhaps nobody gets excited about cleaning the garage. But associate the task with something that *does* excite you—making room for your family's bicycles, having a place to paint, or finding Aunt Thelma's long-lost butterfly collection—and your purpose becomes clear.

So it goes with deep work. Remembering how your project will help your team meet its goals or how your hard work helps you live in a place you love shifts the way you relate to your work. Resistance, maybe even resentment, softens. You see the bigger picture and why the work matters. This makes you more resilient when distractions pop up.

WELCOME THE "IT'S NOT EASY."

You're reading this because you want more happiness, right? Because the way things are doesn't feel like the way you want them to be? But admit it…you've had some moments where you've thought, "I'll never break that habit" or "When will I find time for *that?*"

Ah, resistance. It feels like one of the brain's strongest tendencies. Getting out of automatic routines does seem to take some work.

The first step to a better way is to get excited about the challenge. If you were training for a marathon or looking to perfect your curveball, you'd know you had some heavy lifting ahead.

It's the same when you're training your brain. Get as excited about that as you would about approaching that finish line or seeing the batter swing and miss. You're going to get stronger! More productive! Build mental strength! Map paths that make future changes easier! See challenge as opportunity: a way to win the lasting satisfaction of getting *good* at something new. That thought alone can weaken the tug of the usual distractions.

PREP

Sitting down for a deep work session? Plot your course. Outline. Schedule breaks. Set up your work area as if you were planning a ritual. You may not have to do these things forever, but as you're weaning away from distractions and deepening your work, preparation is low-hanging fruit.

Every navigator knows that preparedness is the key to success. Polar explorer Ernest Shackleton, whose life was largely marked by restlessness and failure, ultimately found his greatest victory through preparation. When ice froze around his Antarctica-bound ship, taking it eight hundred miles off course and crushing it after ten months of helpless drifting, his foresight paid off. His organizational skills and near-obsessive planning ensured his crew of twenty-eight sailors all survived the grueling endeavor. Anything else and they would never have made it home.

RECLAIM THE UPPER HAND

Once again, the things that distract us were often *designed* to distract us. Apps, casinos, video games, ads, political campaigns, TV serials: the people who create them are experts at using "hooks" to activate dopamine-fueled craving in your brain. They know how to keep us hanging, to get us to click just one more time. They often use science to lure us in. Well, we can use our own science to resist!

Start by shifting your thoughts. Stop blaming or criticizing yourself. Move from "I'm so distractible" to "This app was engineered to distract me and make me want to keep coming back." That's different from blaming the tech (or the casino, the TV show, or whatever it is that feels like it's taking charge of you). Seeing yourself as a victim won't help you kick the habit.

Understanding you're being hacked, though? That helps you look more objectively at what's happening around you. That awareness gives you options. You can summon the steps listed above to start deepening your focus on something that motivates you even more than what that ad, game, or channel tries to insist you want. They may be good...but *you're* better.

FOCUS ON PROCESS

Taking things step-by-step is the only way anything ever happens. Back in 1983, when Steve Jobs was passionately focused on creating the first Mac, he sent everyone on his team a printed page with a clear message to keep at their desks:

How is the decision you're making right now helping us to ship the greatest personal computer the world has ever known on January 24, 1984?

That message directed his team to make each step matter. Micro-decisions and small, steady prioritizations shape the path to success. Each moment will offer us trade-offs: power through or look away? Do the right thing or the easy one? Most of us already know how we feel when we choose the second option.

The JOURNEY is the REWARD.
—STEVE JOBS

STICK WITH IT

Distraction has been training us for a *long* time. Learning new ways takes work, so the first steps toward change can feel fruitless or frustrating.

Keep practicing. Resistance is part of the process. See it for what it is: not a dead end, but a roadblock you can get around. Keep pushing, and remind yourself, "It's normal for this to feel hard," or "It sure feels different without those easy distractions—but I'm working toward a deeper reward."

About Multitasking

Sorry, but multitasking is a hoax. If you think you're good at managing a lot of details concurrently, you're probably actually good at one of these things:

TASK SWITCHING

You may be extra efficient at shifting smoothly between different brain modalities. If so, congratulations. But don't trick yourself. Moving between activities taxes the brain, causing fatigue, confusion, and agitation—hardly paths to happiness. It may seem to only take a moment to check email or peek in on your "likes," but you pay the cost in time and attention as your brain works its way back to what you were doing before.

INTERWEAVING

We can frame several seemingly disconnected things into a bigger picture, seeing them as a whole. If calling the doctor, warming a bottle, finding your keys, and getting ready to head out into the rainstorm are all part of "find out what's wrong with the baby," your brain can organize these things into a unified task.

But it's expensive, in brain terms. Orchestration like this happens in the PFC, that glucose- and oxygen-hungry area. It only works well for short periods of time. We can prolong its use in critical situations, but we'll be depleted (literally brain drained) afterward.

In this case, the worried parent should be extra careful while driving, because a tired PFC doesn't integrate complex information well. And they shouldn't be surprised by exhaustion, cravings, or fragile emotions when they finally get the little one back home. Executing complex tasks, especially under stress, is draining work.

We *can*, however, multitask when we're doing multiple routine activities. That's how we walk and chew gum at the same time. We can also balance routine physical activities with certain mental work.

Though this is not without cost, as the rise of accidents related to distracted driving (and even walking!) shows. Researchers at Harvard learned that drivers who multitasked while driving were as likely to tailgate, veer, or brake too late as drivers under the influence of alcohol. Talking on the phone, it turns out, is as dangerous as drunk driving. Be aware of this brain reality. How can you use your new knowledge to increase not only focus, but safety?

Everyday Mindfulness

Welcome that *om* moment and fully tune in to your inner calm. Breaking the noise habit is one of the best ways to train our brains to focus. Stillness and quiet can also shine light on a deeper sense of what matters to us: our purpose, our priorities, and the things that bring us joy.

Meditation isn't about getting rid of thoughts. It's about mastering how we respond to them: learning not to chase them or let them chase us, which we often do in routine mode. It's about bringing our mind, our Watcher, our awareness—call it what you will—to our thoughts and actions.

This practice can take many forms. In fact, the reason people meditate is to learn to bring mindful practices "off the cushion" and into everyday life.

Breath. In.

The fact that meditation often involves intentional breath is yet another example of ancient wisdom pointing to brain-aware behavior. Mindful breathing, it turns out, changes our brains. As Christina Zelano, a professor at Northwestern's medical school, has proved,

"There's a dramatic difference in brain activity...during inhalation compared with exhalation.

"When you breathe in, we discovered you are stimulating neurons in the olfactory cortex, amygdala, and hippocampus and across the limbic system," Dr. Zelano reports. "When you inhale, you are synchronizing brain oscillations across the limbic network." Her research shows that the rhythm of breath affects activity in the brain areas where emotions and memory are processed.

Mindfulness is about deepening awareness, and you can practice it in any setting. When cooking or eating, focus on the fragrances or textures of the food before you. When out on a walk, connect with your brain as you shift your attention from a distant mountain to the close-up textures on the bark of a tree.

Sit in quiet, or use everyday life to guide your awareness: the choice is yours. *Anything* you do to tune away from the noise and move toward the quieter, more meaningful signal within you guides you to more balance and happiness.

Getting Unstuck

Sometimes the only way to clear a roadblock is to walk around it.

Doing deep work, changing our focus, and building new habits take practice. It can be hard. Sometimes, as the saying goes, we get the bear. Sometimes...well, you know the rest. If it's the warm fuzzy bear of serotonin you're after, remember that even the ancient Greeks knew satisfaction took long-term work and lots of practice.

Sometimes we get stuck. We run out of steam. Or something

happens that takes us jarringly off path. Or we simply need more than our current brain state seems to offer.

ADAPT what is useful, reject what is useless, and ADD what is specifically your own.
—BRUCE LEE, ACTOR AND MARTIAL ARTS MASTER

Don't panic. You have choices, ones that reinforce your happiness practice and cross over to many other life scenarios.

SHIFT GEARS

If you're working on a computer, get out your pen and paper. Maybe walk around talking about the problem. Record that, and listen back. This will help you organize and map the information in different ways. Who knows? Maybe you and your brain will map your way to an answer.

TALK NICE

To yourself, that is. Avoid self-criticism. Our subconscious mind has a way of pointing the problem back at us when we hit a skid. If you try to change a habit or do everything you can to focus and it still doesn't work, give yourself a break. Reflect on why you're stuck and what skills you can call on to move forward. What *can* you do? Encourage yourself as you would a treasured friend. You may see your next steps in a whole new light.

REPLENISH

Take a moment to make sure you're taking extra good care of your body. Your roadblock may simply be a tired PFC, depleted by hunger, fatigue, stress, or other brain drains. Get up. Stretch. Get a glass of water or something nourishing to eat. Meditate, even for ten minutes. Remember, your brain and your body are part of one system. Caring for one creates good for the other.

OPTIMIZE FOR AHA

"Aha moments" happen by surprise, as the name suggests, when two or more previously unconnected ideas find each other through a new connection and, *whoosh*, a new brain pathway is formed. You can almost feel it—but you can't force it.

To increase the likeliness of an aha moment, shift gears. Seek sensory input that's different from what you've been trying. There's a reason so many people get their best ideas in the shower: the sound and feel of water, the warmth, calm, or maybe even the ions shift something in the brain and open it to insight. You have to *collect* the right dots before you can connect them. Go find yourself a few more dots.

TAKE A BREAK

You can run screaming from the roadblock or see it as a workout partner. Either may work, but one (guess which?) tends to work better. Plan a hike, or even a walk around the block, and tell your brain, "Time for a clean slate," or "How about a nature break?"

Whatever you do—running a load of laundry, reading, or going for a leg-pumping bike ride—do it attentively. Absorb yourself in it. Watch the details. Focus on *how* you're doing what you're doing.

Often, we do the opposite. We take the stress of a roadblock with us and go through the motions of doing something else. Yet awakening your senses by creating a completely different experience refreshes the brain. It may replenish the idea supply in the very brain areas you need to get around that block.

As we learn to take mindful, intentional charge of how we use our brains, we direct ourselves increasingly toward choices and activities that bring more satisfaction—and help strengthen our highest-level cognitive abilities. *That*, it turns out, fuels satisfaction in and of itself. And things get even better when we use our new mastery to activate our brains.

Navigating the Invisible
TAKING CONTROL OF THE BODY'S MOST AUTONOMOUS PROCESSES

Breath and working with our body changes our psychology so we become happy, strong, and healthy.
—WIM HOF, MIND CONTROL MASTER

It would be one thing if Wim Hof hiked to the top of Czechia's highest peak in −27°F weather, wearing only shorts, all alone. Then you could call him an outlier: someone possessing a mutant layer of insulating fat, a mind of absolute steel, or a very unusual metabolism.

But he didn't hike alone. In multiple summits of that peak, Hof brought companions: dozens of them, women and men, early twenties through midsixties, from all corners of the globe. They all climbed, lively and smiling, astonishing border guards and medical professionals as they gleefully reached the top and celebrated (one group danced the Harlem Shuffle), clad, basically, in beachwear.

Some say it's Hof's charismatic personality. "Just being in his presence inspired us to accomplish things we never would have normally done," said one climber.

But watch Hof, and you'll learn it's something more.

Hof teaches his devotees an unusual breathing technique: deep breaths with partial exhales followed by prolonged holds. It's easy to learn, and the proof starts fast. After a short orientation, Hof guides his mentees into increasingly long cold-water plunges or sessions of sprawling nearly naked in snow. Almost from the get-go, his students express awe at not feeling cold.

After four days, they're ready to scale an icy mountain.

If this were only Hof, you'd think he was a hoax. But countless scientists have monitored his abilities, marveling at how he can stand, say, in a huge box of ice for nearly two hours while maintaining his body's core temperature.

Or how he climbed to twenty-two thousand feet at Mount Everest, reached the summit of Mount Kilimanjaro in only two days; ran a full marathon above the Arctic Circle, clad only in shoes and shorts; and aced another marathon in Africa's Namib Desert (where temperatures often reach 113°F) without drinking water. Hof achieved each of these feats under rigorous medical and scientific supervision.

How does he do it? And how does he teach others to join the "fun"? Turns out, Hof uses the power of his mind to take control of the invisible: the unconscious, and normally autonomous, brain regions that control the body and the central nervous system.

"Breathing and intention change things," he has said. "They get us beneath fear, back to the unconditioned nature and inner power we all have. We learn to control what's within ourselves, reclaiming our true happiness, health, and strength. It's not philosophical. It's chemical. And anyone can do it."

Hof may have mastered a form of mind control also cultivated by Tibetan Tummo meditators. In their practice, breath, visualization, and a shutdown of mental activity let them convert body energy into heat. Experiments on these meditators documented temperature increases of nearly 12°F in their fingers and toes and noteworthy changes to core body temperature.

Hof's mastery, though, goes beyond temperature control. Under intense medical scrutiny, he has been injected with bacterial by-products that ordinarily cause extreme chills, aches, and fever. As doctors prodded and measured, Hof took control and suppressed his body's reaction.

What's more, twelve trainees joined him in that adventure, also avoiding illness.

There's something to the breathing that stimulates an adrenaline response, but Hof says it's more than that. He believes we all have more control of our autonomous systems than we've been conditioned to believe.

"Everyone is able to do much more than is thought of," he insists.

"Enlightenment is a state of happiness and health, and it's not as distant as we're told it is.

"We can learn to control our body from within our body. This is our natural ability. Anyone can do this. My dream is to show everyone how."

Activating

Practice *Kuleana*: accept your personal responsibility and sacred duty. Practice *Ho'ohana*: work with intent and purpose. Practice *Imi Ola*: seek your best life. Our purpose in life is to seek its highest form. Pursue the value of mission and vision.

—VALUES OF *ALOHA*, TRADITIONAL HAWAI'IAN WISDOM

THE BRAIN IS A powerful instrument—an extraordinary powerhouse ready to help us navigate nearly any situation life might bring our way.

Yet there's something even more powerful than this three-pound marvel: *you*. When you direct this "most complicated object in the known universe," working *with* your brain, you're at your best. But as you've learned, it takes new intentions, actions, and attitudes master this ability.

The grass is ALWAYS greener where you WATER it.

—UNKNOWN

In Charge, On Purpose

What do you want more than the easy indulgences dangled out there to distract you from your path?

How will you get there? What's the first step, whatever it might be, that points you in that direction?

And why do you want that achievement or experience? What makes you excited, curious, or hungry to pursue it?

Ask yourself these questions and listen openly to what comes up. Really...listen. Don't be surprised if a voice inside you tries to shut your excitement down. Remember, the brain tends to preserve the thoughts and actions you've already taken, resisting the effort and perceived risks often associated with new thoughts. Don't worry if that happens. It's normal.

But keep asking, and stay mindful of the answers. Somewhere in them you'll find clues to what really matters to you. Something in your answers may spark embers of empathy or strike chords of passion. What you hear may help you identify something you want to make better, in the world or in your life, through intention and contribution.

It might be a small thing. We live in a time where big problems overwhelm us, so we often expect ourselves to think big. It's easy to forget that small actions can spark big changes.

Your answer might point you to creating a loving home or to supporting people who face obstacles. It may be as simple as creating art or telling stories that build understanding (or break down walls). Maybe it points to curing a disease, slowing climate change, or facing a political problem in a way that visibly changes the world.

But it doesn't need to be. Things as small as bringing renewable bags to the grocery store, de-escalating an angry conversation, or telling your child how you admire the way they said thank you at dinner: any of those things can align us with purpose.

Any of those things can help change the world.

A lot of people expect their purpose to be a job title, an epic achievement, or maybe something that changes countless lives. It's easy to understand where that expectation might come from, especially in the high-pressure times we all live in. The noise around us glorifies the few who rise to power, wealth, or public acclaim.

Meanwhile, much in the world is held together by the actions of countless people whose essential contributions simply never win acclaim.

That doesn't make those contributions any less important.

"Purpose" doesn't have to be about some large-scale external achievement. It may be about the way you do something—kindly, or as part of a community. It may be about the way you spend time—encouraging others, or being a healthy role model. Perhaps it's about bringing more beauty to the world, through something you create, something you nurture, or simply the way you live. Or even about bringing security and confidence to those you love, which is perhaps one of the greatest purposes of all.

It's a helluva start, being able to RECOGNIZE what makes you happy.

—LUCILLE BALL , GROUNDBREAKING COMEDIENNE

Maybe it is about improving something large scale: aligning with a path you deeply believe in, even if it means risking the ease and approval of a more ordinary life. Whatever it is, learning to listen to yourself, and tuning away from the easy distractions that can scramble our signals of truth, is a first step in tuning in to more

What you DO makes a difference, and you have to DECIDE what kind of difference you want to MAKE.

—JANE GOODALL, WILDLIFE RESEARCHER, ANTHROPOLOGIST, U.N. MESSENGER OF PEACE purpose and satisfaction. It's hard to break free of the noise. Yet it's a time-honored path to greater happiness.

Whether your purpose is to change the world or simply to change *your* world, look inside, and trust what you find there. "Collect the dots" around your deepest wishes and the things that bring you the greatest satisfaction. As your collection grows, the connections, too, will become more clear. We're here to contribute, and our brains know it. And that's what this book is really about: awakening a memory in you that may have gotten lost in all of the noise and distraction of everyday life. You are here for a reason, and your reason is worthy. Your happiness stems from knowing and acting on that, even as distractions dangle around you.

The journey of happiness is mapped by your brain, but it's directed by *you*. As you recognize invisible or routine modes and shift to intentional thinking, you are already clearing your path to success.

Now, the journey begins. Between you and your brain, you have all it takes to find what you're looking for.

An Appropriate Response
THE MINDFUL VISION OF ZEN BUDDHIST PAMELA WEISS

The Buddhist path offers a powerful set of practices for engaging with the world in ways that enrich happiness and deepen our experience of purpose, perspective, and possibility.

—PAMELA WEISS, TEACHER, EXECUTIVE
COACH, LEADERSHIP GUIDE

Back in the eighties, Pamela Weiss was a recent college graduate and newly-minted professional working for a health-care consulting practice. She had a mission: improving the quality of medical care to people like herself, a Type 1 diabetic since age ten.

Her illness had blocked her from lifelong dreams of travel and adventure. Yet, determined as she was to fight the condition, her job wasn't cutting it. Spreadsheets and endless reports were not what she had in mind. She was bored, frustrated, and dissatisfied.

That's when Weiss discovered San Francisco Zen Center. She was taken aback by the kindness and peace of the community she met there. *Whatever they've got, I want*, she thought. She became so drawn in, she decided to forgo graduate school and dedicate herself to the rigor of Zen Buddhist training.

That was over thirty years ago. Today, Weiss is a Buddhist teacher whose work is rooted in the psychology and discipline of Buddhist practice. "Most of us move through life wanting pleasant experiences and resisting unpleasant ones," she explains. "Largely, 'I like it' or 'I don't like it' defines our experience.

"This may work temporarily. But it doesn't last. Buddhism teaches that becoming objectively present to our moment-to-moment experience allows us to shift from reacting habitually to responding appropriately."

Appropriate response is a term from one of Weiss's favorite Zen teaching stories. "A student visits an honored teacher in his final hours," she shares. "He asks, 'What is the teaching of your entire lifetime?' Likely, the student expected a big, enlightening answer. But in the spare simplicity of Zen wisdom, the master simply replied, 'An appropriate response.'"

The term is also the name of the leadership development

practice Weiss founded, elevating principled, mindful leadership in some of Silicon Valley's best known companies. "'Appropriate response' is the essence of what so many of us seek—and seek to provide," she explains. "We all face struggles and dilemmas. Life can feel overwhelming, even though we are smart, capable people. What we need are practices and perspectives that allow us to meet the complexity with clarity, courage, and kindness."

Her current work focuses on shaping a new model for leadership based on the Buddhist concept of a Bodhisattva. "*Bodhisattva* is a term bursting with richness and meaning," she says. "*Bodhi* means awake, enlightened, or wise. *Sattva* means sentient being. *Bodhisattva leadership* means having the awareness to master the perceptions and feelings of the human experience so we can be helpful to others, sharing wisdom and kindness in skillful ways."

Her goal? To have the term *bodhisattva* shape a new narrative for leaders of all kinds. "Bodhisattvas understand our place in the web of all being," she explains. "Our health as humans is intricately tied to the health of our planet, the health of all others. Bodhisattva leadership is fueled by the wish to increase this health and well-being, alleviating suffering and expanding freedom and joy. My vision is for the word 'bodhisattva' to define our sense of leadership within the next decade. Given the complexity and divisiveness of our time, I see this as an essential path.

"Buddhist teaching and the bodhisattva path offer a framework for realizing genuine contentment," Weiss concludes. "Happiness means true satisfaction: beyond fleeting moments of pleasant experience. My aspiration is to make this understanding available as widely as I can."

Taking CHARGE

Your time is limited, so don't waste it living someone else's life… Don't let the noise of others' opinions drown out your own inner voice. And most important, have the courage to follow your heart and intuition. They somehow already know what you truly want to become.

—STEVE JOBS

When I was in grade school, they told me to write down what I wanted to be when I grew up. I wrote down "happy." They told me I didn't understand the assignment. I told them they didn't understand life.

—UNKNOWN

AS THE DEEPLY SATISFYING journey of writing this book was coming to a close, I stepped outside for a breath of fresh air. A neighbor was out for a walk, and we said hello.

She was visibly sad. She started talking about her frustration and feelings of helplessness as she thought about the many difficult conditions in today's world. "It's all so hard," she said. "And there's nothing I can do to make a difference."

One thing I've always appreciated about this neighbor is how she makes eye contact. A former professional dancer, her warm brown eyes and wavy white hair make her lovely to look at. Yet her eyes were sad as she spoke about all that troubled her. It was clear she'd been thinking about this—and her sense of helplessness—a lot.

"It kills me to think there's nothing I can do," she said, a tinge of anger in her voice.

As I looked at her, I wondered what my mirror neurons were doing and if that was oxytocin I felt activating my sense of empathy.

I could have reacted. My automatic mode would gladly have jumped in, egging her on and perhaps escalating the despair. "I know!" I could have said. "It makes me so angry that…" inserting whatever opinion or news story seemed to add to the sense of outrage.

But I slowed down and found a different response. "You *are* doing something," I told her. She looked curious. "Whenever I talk with you, I notice how you make eye contact. You really connect. I'll bet you do that often when you interact with people."

She wavered, glancing away. After a moment, though, she looked back, nodding. "People do seem to say that from time to time."

So I gave her a mini lecture—exactly the type of thing that tends to annoy my sons—on mirror neurons. I told her how simple things like eye contact actually helped shift people from routine, automatic patterns and into more awareness. And how awareness can activate the parts of our brains that improve mood, social connection, and impulse control. Her kind eye contact, I suggested, might help others treat someone else more kindly, catalyzing a virtuous chain of "pass it on."

Her gaze softened. Her expression looked more hopeful. She reached over and squeezed my hand.

(Take that, sons!)

"It reminds me," she said, a hint of excitement in her voice, "of that thing Gandhi said. You know: 'Be the change you want to see in the world.'"

"Exactly," I agreed.

She twinkled, then shrugged. "If it's good enough for Gandhi, I guess it's good enough for me."

My LIFE is my MESSAGE.

—MAHATMA GANDHI

It's never too late to get back in charge, as my lovely neighbor illustrates. If I'd thought it was too late ten years ago, I would never have written this book.

Around that time, my coworker Marlene shared a saying she'd learned from her grandmother, who had emigrated to the United States from China. It goes like this:

"When you stand at the bottom of a mountain and look up, all you see are the things that block your path. Yet when you reach the top and look down, you will know: one hundred paths would have brought you to that place."

Happiness, real happiness, is calling you. You can bring it to your life. And everything on your path so far, even when you least believe it, has brought you to the place where you are ready to find more of it.

We think we have to be fearless to move forward, toward happiness and the deeper satisfaction we seek.

Sure. Except *fearless* is actually two words in one, and when you take them apart, you get a new message:

FEAR LESS.

That is truly all it takes: fear less. Even a little bit less. Summon your Watcher. Smile at your threat state or automatic mode, and reassure it. Tell it, "Go on break. I've got this."

And then take a step. You, after all, have the most powerful object in the known universe on your side. It's watching *you*, this very moment, ready to learn from what you do next.

Whatever you choose, it is ready to help you do more of. It's on your side. And now you know how to work with it too. It's ready, and so are you.

Welcome to your first step toward more happiness—and the satisfaction you deserve.

Recommended
READING

If this exploration of your brain and its role in your happiness has sparked your interest, great news! Resources to deepen your learning abound.

For an easy-to-understand, actionable guide to "overcoming distraction, regaining focus, and working smarter all day long," consider *Your Brain at Work* by Dr. David Rock. This general introduction to various systems within the brain explores a series of real-life challenges faced by a typical family, offering scenarios for how they solved problems before and after they understood the workings of specific parts of their brains. More at neuroleadership.com.

Dr. Carol Dweck's excellent *Mindset* looks at the attitudinal shifts that can redirect our thinking into growth-oriented new directions, harnessing the power of neuroplasticity to guide learning and growth. While her work often applies to education, it's every bit as valuable for adults. I highly recommend this book and the information she shares on her website, mindsetworks.com.

For a fascinating look into the "Watcher's" experience of the brain, Dr. Jill Bolte Taylor's *My Stroke of Insight* offers an eye-opening real-life narrative. A respected neuroanatomist, Dr. Taylor received a unique journey into understanding the brain as she experienced, and worked to recover from, a large-scale stroke. Her TED talk on the subject and website, mystrokeofinsight.com, offer fascinating insights on a brain scientist's discovery of her own brain—including a few surprises—through her medical journey and recovery.

And, of course, I keep an active list of updates, new learning, and speaking engagements, among other things, on my website: ellenleanse.com.

ACKNOWLEDGMENTS

I could not have been either confident or accurate writing about the brain in scientific terms without the fastidious review provided by systems neuroscientist Sarah Eagleman, PhD. Her knowledge and attention to detail made the sections of this book most centered on the brain more accurate, and thus more useful to readers. I'm extremely grateful for her contributions, her many helpful insights, and the pleasure of working with her. Any inconsistencies, lack of clarity, or errors in explanations are mine, not hers.

Thanks, too, to Buddhist practitioner and teacher Pamela Weiss for her inspiration and contributions. As the Chief Wisdom Officer of Appropriate Response, Pamela has helped enlighten senior executives at some of the world's most venerated companies. She's also guided countless learners, including me, in applying the Buddha's teachings to everyday life.

Gratitude as well to friends including Roz Savage, MBE; Wade Roush, PhD; Susan Spinrad Esterly, PhD; Anil Ananthaswamy; Shaherose Charania; Derek Skaletsky;

Chrissy Farr; Serena Malkani; the Jaffer family; Victor D. Lombard; George Woods Baker; Krista Donaldson, MSE, PhD; Adrienne F. Huesca; Cy Hoss; Pavlina Yanakleva; Lindsay Holden; Avish Bhama; Vicki Reece; Mac; and Monique and Travis Giggy for their encouragement and helpful candor. I owe the same to my community at Stanford, DENT, and beyond, and above all to my family members: my sons, siblings, nieces, and nephews.

And tremendous thanks to Meg Gibbons, my editor and true partner at Sourcebooks, for seeing the light and helping it shine.

About the
AUTHOR

Ellen Petry Leanse teaches, coaches, speaks, and lives with conviction that brain-aware practices elevate mastery and satisfaction in all aspects of life. Today she focuses on sharing these practices through her work as a leadership coach, as an author, and as a globally followed keynote speaker.

A thirty-five-year veteran of Silicon Valley, Ellen spent nine years at Apple, where she served on the Macintosh launch team and created the company's first online presence (1985). Since then, she has worked at or with companies including Google, Facebook, Microsoft, and dozens of others to make innovation more meaningful and understandable to technology users everywhere.

Ellen has contributed to or been quoted in publications

including *Time, Inc.*, *Business Insider*, *Vogue*, *Fast Company*, and many others. Her article on language, gender, and the word "just" has received more than five million views and been referenced in dozens of response pieces. She's also spoken about the science of happiness on *The Today Show*, CNN, *Secular Buddhism*, and dozens of well-known podcasts. A TEDx speaker, Ellen's view on "Happiness by Design" has helped viewers everywhere understand the ease and benefits of bringing gratitude practices to their lives.

The mother of three adult sons, Ellen lives and works in Northern California.

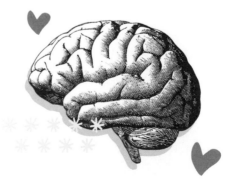

NEW! Only from Simple Truths®

IGNITE READS
spark impact in just one hour

IGNITE READS IS A NEW SERIES OF 1-HOUR READS WRITTEN BY WORLD-RENOWNED EXPERTS!

These captivating books will help you become the best version of yourself, allowing for new opportunities in your personal and professional life. Accelerate your career and expand your knowledge with these powerful books written on today's hottest ideas.

TRENDING BUSINESS AND PERSONAL GROWTH TOPICS

 Read in an hour or less

Leading experts and authors

 Bold design and captivating content